WHO MADE YOU?

WHO MADE YOU?

Theology, Science, and Human Responsibility

Alfred H. Howell

CONVERGENCE

A Series Founded, Planned, and Edited
by Ruth Nanda Anshen

PRAEGER

New York
Westport, Connecticut
London

Library of Congress Cataloging-in-Publication Data

Howell, Alfred H.
  Who made you? / Alfred H. Howell.
    p.   cm.—(Convergence)
  Bibliography: p.
  Includes index.
  ISBN 0-275-93293-1 (alk. paper).
  ISBN 0-275-93294-X (pbk. : alk. paper)
  1. Man.   2. Creation—Controversial literature.   3. Evolution.
4. Revelation—Controversial literature.   5. Rationalism.
I. Title.   II. Series: Covergence (New York, N.Y.)
BL2715.H65   1989
210—dc20   89-30018

Library of Congress Catalog Card Number: 89-30018
ISBN: 0-275-93293-1 (hb)
        0-275-93294-X (pb)

First published in 1989

Praeger Publishers, One Madison Avenue, New York, NY 10010
A division of Greenwood Press, Inc.

Printed in the United States of America

The paper used in this book complies with the Permanent
Paper Standard issued by the National Information Standards
Organization (Z39.48-1984).

10 9 8 7 6 5 4 3 2 1

To all clear-thinking scholars and scientists,
present and future,
tirelessly working to remove barriers
of ignorance, myth, and superstition
from the paths of mankind,
and
To far-seeing, wise, humane leadership
which will guide man beside still waters
and restore his soul

CONVERGENCE

A Series Founded, Planned, and Edited by Ruth Nanda Anshen

BOOKS IN THE CONVERGENCE SERIES

Contents

Convergence

Ruth Nanda Anshen

"There is no use trying," said Alice; "one *can't* believe impossible things."

"I dare say you haven't had much practice," said the Queen, "When I was your age, I always did it for half an hour a day. Why, sometimes I've believed as many as six impossible things before breakfast."

This commitment is an inherent part of human nature and an aspect of our creativity. Each advance of science brings increased comprehension and appreciation of the nature, meaning, and wonder of the creative forces that move the cosmos and created man. Such openness and confidence lead to faith in the reality of possibility and eventually to the following truth: "The mystery of the universe is its comprehensibility."

When Einstein uttered that challenging statement, he could have been speaking about our relationship with the universe. The old division of the Earth and the Cosmos into objective processes in space and time and mind in which they are mirrored is no longer a suitable starting point for understanding the universe, science, or ourselves. Science now begins to focus on the convergence of man and nature, on the framework which makes us, as living beings, dependent parts of nature and simultaneously makes nature the object of our thoughts and actions. Scientists can no longer confront the universe as objective observers. Science recognizes the participation of man with the universe. Speaking quantitatively, the universe is largely indifferent to what happens in man. Speaking qualitatively, nothing happens in man that does not have a bearing on the elements which constitute the universe. This gives cosmic significance to the person.

Nevertheless, all facts are not born free and equal. There exists a hierarchy of facts in relation to a hierarchy of values. To arrange the facts rightly, to differentiate the important from the trivial, to see their bearing in relation to each other and to evaluational criteria, requires a judgment which is intuitive as well as empirical. We need meaning in addition to information. Accuracy is not the same as truth.

Our hope is to overcome the cultural *hubris* in which we have been living. The scientific method, the technique of analyzing, explaining, and classifying, has demonstrated its inherent limitations. They arise because, by its intervention, science presumes to alter and fashion the object of its investigation. In reality, method and object can no longer be separated. The outworn Cartesian, scientific world view has ceased to be scientific in the most profound sense of the word, for a common bond links us all—man, animal, plant, and galaxy—in the unitary principle of all reality. For the self without the universe is empty.

This universe of which we human beings are particles may be defined as a living, dynamic process of unfolding. It is a breathing universe, its respiration being only one of the many rhythms of its life. It is evolution itself. Although what we observe may seem to be a community of separate, independent units, in actuality these units are made up of subunits, each with a life of its own, and the subunits constitute smaller living entities. At no level in the hierarchy of nature is independence a reality. For that which lives and constitutes matter, whether organic or inorganic, is dependent on discrete entities that, gathered together, form aggregates of new units which interact in support of one another and become an unfolding event, in constant motion, with ever-increasing complexity and intricacy of their organization.

Are there goals in evolution? Or are there only discernible patterns? Certainly there is a law of evolution by which we can explain the emergence of forms capable of activities which are indeed novel. Examples may be said to be the origin of life, the emergence of individual consciousness, and the appearance of language.

The hope of the concerned authors in Convergence is that they will show that evolution and development are interchangeable and that the entire system of the interweaving of man, nature, and the universe constitutes a living totality. Man is searching for his legitimate place in this unity, this cosmic scheme of things. The meaning of this cosmic scheme—if indeed we can impose meaning on the mystery and majesty of nature—and the extent to which we can assume responsibility in it as uniquely intelligent beings, are supreme questions for which this series seeks an answer.

Inevitably, toward the end of a historical period, when thought and custom have petrified into rigidity and when the elaborate machinery of civilization opposes and represses our more noble qualities, life stirs again beneath the hard surface. Nevertheless, this attempt to define the purpose of Convergence is set forth with profound trepidation. We are living in a period of extreme darkness. There is moral atrophy, destructive radiation within us, as we watch the collapse of values hitherto cherished—but now betrayed. We seem to be face to face with an apocalyptic destiny. The anomie, the chaos, surrounding us produces an almost lethal disintegration of the person, as well as ecological and demographic disaster. Our situation is desperate. And there is no glossing over the deep and unresolved tragedy that fills our lives. Science now begins to question its premises and tells us not only what *is*, but what *ought* to be; *pre*scribing in addition to *de*scribing the realities of life, reconciling order and hierarchy.

My introduction to Convergence is not to be construed as a prefatory essay to each individual volume. These few pages attempt to set forth the general aim and purpose of this series. It is my hope that this statement will provide the reader with a new orientation in his thinking, one more specifically defined by these scholars who have been invited to participate in this intellectual, spiritual, and moral endeavor so desperately needed in our time. These scholars recognize the relevance of the nondiscursive experience of life which the discursive, analytical method alone is unable to convey.

The authors invited to the Convergence Series acknowledge a structural kinship between subject and object, between living and nonliving matter, the immanence of the past energizing the present and thus bestowing a promise for the future. This kinship has long been sensed and experienced by mystics. Saint Francis of Assisi described with extraordinary beauty the truth that the more we know about nature, its unity with all life, the more we realize that we are one family, summoned to acknowledge the intimacy of our familial ties with the universe. At one time we were so anthropomorphic as to exclude as inferior such other aspects of our relatives as animals, plants, galaxies, or other species—even inorganic matter. This only exposed our provincialism. Then we believed there were borders beyond which we could not, must not, trespass. These frontiers have never existed. Now we are beginning to recognize, even take pride in, our neighbors in the cosmos.

Human thought has been formed through centuries of man's consciousness, by perceptions and meanings that relate us to nature. The smallest living entity, be it a molecule or a particle, is at the same time present in the structure of the Earth and all its inhabitants, whether human or manifesting themselves in the multiplicity of other forms of life.

Today we are beginning to open ourselves to this evolved experience of consciousness. We keenly realize that man has intervened in the evolutionary process. The future is contingent, not completely prescribed, except for the immediate necessity to evaluate in order to live a life of integrity. The specific gravity of the burden of change has moved from genetic to cultural evolution. Genetic evolution itself has taken millions of years; cultural evolution is a child of no more than twenty or thirty thousand years. What will be the future of our evolutionary course? Will it be cyclical in the classical sense? Will it be linear in the modern sense? Yet we know that the laws of nature are not linear. Certainly, life is more than mere endless repetition. We must restore the importance of each moment, each deed. This is impossible if the future is nothing but a mechanical extrapolation of the past. Dignity becomes possible only with choice. The choice is ours.

In this light, evolution shows man arisen by a creative power inherent in the universe. The immense ancestral effort that has borne man invests him with a cosmic responsibility. Michelangelo's image of Adam created at God's command becomes a more intelligent symbol of man's position in the world than does a description of man as a chance aggregate of atoms or cells. Each successive stage of emergence is more comprehensive, more meaningful, more fulfilling, and more converging, than the last. Yet a higher faculty must always operate through the levels that are below it. The higher faculty must enlist the laws controlling the lower levels in the service of higher principles, and the lower level which enables the higher one to operate through it will always limit the scope of these operations, even menacing them with possible failure. All our higher endeavors must work through our lower forms and are necessarily exposed thereby to corruption. We may thus recognize the cosmic roots of tragedy and our fallible human condition. Language itself as the power of universals, is the basic expression of man's ability to transcend his environment and to transmute tragedy into a moral and spiritual triumph.

This relationship, this convergence, of the higher with the lower applies again when an upper level, such as consciousness or freedom, endeavors to reach beyond itself. If no higher level can be accounted for by the operation of a lower level, then no effort of ours can be truly creative in the sense of establishing a higher principle not intrinsic to our initial condition. And establishing such a principle is what all great art, great thought, and great action must aim at. This is indeed how these efforts have built up the heritage in which our lives continue to grow.

Has man's intelligence broken through the limits of his own powers? Yes and no. Inventive efforts can never fully account for their success, but the story of man's evolution testifies to a creative power that goes beyond that which we can account for in ourselves. This power can make us surpass ourselves. We exercise some of it in the simple act of acquiring knowledge and holding it to be true. For, in doing so, we strive for intellectual control over things outside ourselves, in spite of our manifest incapacity to justify this hope. The greatest efforts of the human mind amount to no more than this. All such acts impose an obligation to strive for the ostensibly impossible, representing man's search for the fulfillment of those ideals which, for the moment, seem to be beyond his reach. For the good of a moral act is inherent in the act itself and has the power to ennoble the person who performs it. Without this moral ingredient there is corruption.

The origins of one person can be envisaged by tracing that person's family tree all the way back to the primeval specks of protoplasm in which his first origins lie. The history of the family tree converges with everything that has contributed to the making of a human being. This segment of evolution is on a par with the history of a fertilized egg developing into a mature person, or the history of a plant growing from a seed; it includes everything that caused that person, or that plant, or that animal, or even that star in a galaxy, to come into existence. Natural selection plays no part in the evolution of a single human being. We do not include in the mechanism of growth the possible adversities which did not befall it and hence did not prevent it. The same principle of development holds for the evolution of a single human being; nothing is gained in understanding this evolution by considering the adverse chances which might have prevented it.

In our search for a reasonable cosmic view, we turn in the first place to common understanding. Science largely relies for its subject matter on a common knowledge of things. Concepts of life and death, plant and animal, health and sickness, youth and age, mind and body, machine and technical processes, and other innumerable and equally important things are commonly known. All these concepts apply to complex entities, whose reality is called into question by a theory of knowledge which claims that the entire universe should ultimately be represented in all its aspects by the physical laws governing the inanimate substrate of nature. "Technological inevitability" has alienated our relationship with nature, with work, with other human beings, with ourselves. Judgment, decision, and freedom of choice, in other words *knowledge* which contains a moral imperative, cannot be ordered in the form that some technological scientists believe. For there is no mechanical ordering, no exhaustive set of permutations or combinations that can perform the task. The power which man has achieved through technology has been transformed into spiritual and moral impotence. Without the insight into the nature of *being*, more important than *doing*, the soul of man is imperiled. And those self-transcendent ends that ultimately confer dignity, meaning, and identity on man and his life constitute the only final values worth pursuing. The pollution of consciousness is the result of mere technological efficiency. In addition, the authors in this series recognize that the computer in itself can process information—not meaning. Performance is now substituted for thought; the doer substituted for the thinker. Thus we see on the stage of life no moral actors, only anonymous events.

Our new theory of knowledge, as the authors in this series try to demonstrate, rejects this claim and restores our respect for the immense range of common knowledge acquired by our experience of convergence. Starting from here, we sketch out our cosmic perspective by exploring the wider implications of the fact that all knowledge is acquired and possessed by relationship, coalescence, convergence.

We identify a person's physiognomy by depending on our awareness of features that we are unable to specify, and this amounts to a convergence in the features of a person for the purpose of comprehending their joint meaning. We are also able to read in the features and behavior of a person the presence of moods, the gleam of intelligence, the response to animals or a sunset or a fugue by Bach, the signs of sanity, human responsibility, and experience. At a lower level, we comprehend by a similar mechanism the body of a person and understand the functions of the physiological mechanism. We know that even physical theories constitute in this way the processes of inanimate nature. Such are the various levels of knowledge acquired and possessed by the experience of convergence.

The authors in this series grasp the truth that these levels form a hierarchy of comprehensive entities. Inorganic matter is comprehended by physical laws; the mechanism of physiology is built on these laws and enlists them in its service. Then, the intelligent behavior of a person relies on the healthy functions of the body and, finally, moral responsibility relies on the faculties of intelligence directing moral acts.

We realize how the operations of machines, and of mechanisms in general, rely on the laws of physics but cannot be explained, or accounted for, by these laws. In a hierarchic sequence of comprehensive levels, each higher level is related to the levels below it in the same way as the operations of a machine are related to the particulars, obeying the laws of physics. We cannot explain the operations of an upper level in terms of the particulars on which its operations rely. Each higher level of integration represents, in this sense, a higher level of existence, not completely accountable by the levels below it, yet including these lower levels implicitly.

In a hierarchic sequence of comprehensive levels, each higher level is known to us by relying on our awareness of the particulars on the level below it. We are conscious of each level by internalizing its particulars and mentally performing the integration that constitutes it. This is how all experience, as well as all knowledge, is based on convergence, and this is how the consecutive stages of convergence form a continuous transition from the understanding of the inorganic, the inanimate, to the comprehension of man's moral responsibility and participation in the totality, the organismic whole, of all reality. The sciences of the subject-object relationship thus pass imperceptibly into the metascience of the convergence of the subject and object interrelationship, mutually altering each other. From the minimum of convergence, exercised in a physical observation, we move without a break to the maximum of convergence, which is a total commitment.

"The last of life, for which the first was made, is yet to come." Thus, Convergence has summoned the world's most concerned thinkers to rediscover the experience of *feeling*, as well as of thought. The convergence of all forms of reality presides over the possible fulfillment of self-awareness—not the isolated, alienated self, but rather the participation in the life process with other lives and other forms of life. Convergence is a cosmic force and may possess liberating powers allowing man to become what he is, capable of freedom, justice, love. Thus man experiences the meaning of grace.

A further aim of this series is not, nor could it be, to disparage science. The authors themselves are adequate witness to this fact. Actually, in viewing the role of science, one arrives at a much more modest judgment of its function in our whole body of knowledge. Original knowledge was probably not acquired by us in the active sense; most of it must have been given to us in the same mysterious way we received our consciousness. As to content and usefulness, scientific knowledge is an infinitesimal fraction of natural knowledge. Nevertheless, it is knowledge whose structure is endowed with beauty because its abstractions satisfy our urge for specific knowledge much more fully than does natural knowledge, and we are justly proud of scientific knowledge because we can call it our own creation. It teaches us clear thinking, and the extent to which clear thinking helps us to order our sensations is a marvel which fills the mind with ever new and increasing admiration and awe. Science now begins to include the realm of human values, lest even the memory of what it means to be human be forgotten. In fact, it may well be that science has reached the limits of the knowable and may now be required to recognize its inability to penetrate into the caprice and the mystery of the soul of the atom.

Organization and energy are always with us, wherever we look, on all levels. At the level of the atom organization becomes indistinguishable from form, from order, from whatever the forces are that held the spinning groups of ultimate particles together in their apparent solidity. And now that we are at the atomic level, we find that modern physics has recognized that these ultimate particles are primarily electrical charges, and that mass is therefore a manifestation of energy. This has often been misinterpreted by idealists as meaning that matter has somehow been magicked away as if by a conjuror's wand. But nothing could be more untrue. It is impossible to transform matter into spirit just by making it thin. Bishop Berkeley's views admit of no refutation but carry no conviction nevertheless. However, something has happened to matter. It was only separated from form because it seemed too simple. Now we realize that, and this is an evolutionary change; we cannot separate them. We are now summoned to cease speaking of form and matter and begin to consider the convergence of organization and energy. For the largest molecule we know and the smallest living particles we know overlap. Such a cooperation, even though far down at the molecular level, cannot but remind us of the voluntary cooperation of individual human beings in maintaining patterns of society at levels of organization far higher. The tasks of energy and organization in the making of the universe and ourselves are far from ended.

No individual destiny can be separated from the destiny of the universe. Alfred North Whitehead has stated that every event, every step or process in the universe, involves both effects from past situations and the anticipation of future potentialities. Basic for this doctrine is the assumption that the course of the universe results from a multiple and never-ending complex of steps developing out of one another. Thus, in spite of all evidence to the contrary, we conclude that there is a continuing and permanent energy of that which is not only man but all life. For not an atom stirs in matter, organic and inorganic, that does not have its cunning duplicate in mind. And faith in the convergence of life with all its multiple manifestations creates its own verification.

We are concerned in this series with the unitary structure of all nature. At the beginning, as we see in Hesiod's *Theogony* and in the Book of Genesis, there was a primal unity, a state of fusion in which, later, all elements become separated but then merge again. How-

ever, out of this unity there emerge, through separation, parts of
opposite elements. These opposites intersect or reunite, in meteoric
phenomena or in individual living things. Yet, in spite of the immense diversity of creation, a profound underlying convergence exists in all nature. And the principle of the conservation of energy
simply signifies that there is a *something* that remains constant. Whatever fresh notions of the world may be given us by future experiments, we are certain beforehand that something remains un-
changed, which we may call *energy*. We now do not say that the law
of nature springs from the invariability of God, but with that curious mixture of arrogance and humility which scientists have learned
to put in place of theological terminology, we say instead that the
law of conservation is the physical expression of the elements by
which nature makes itself understood by us.

The universe is our home. There is no other universe than the
universe of all life including the mind of man, the merging of life
with life. Our consciousness is evolving, the primordial principle of
the unfolding of that which is implied or contained in all matter and
spirit. We ask: Will the central mystery of the cosmos, as well as
man's awareness of and participation in it, be unveiled, although
forever receding, asymptotically? Shall we perhaps be able to see all
things, great and small, glittering with new light and reborn meaning, ancient but now again relevant in an iconic image which is
related to our own time and experience?

The cosmic significance of this panorama is revealed when we
consider it as the stages of an evolution that has achieved the rise of
man and his consciousness. This is the new plateau on which we
now stand. It may seem obvious that the succession of changes,
sustained through a thousand million years, which have transformed
microscopic specks of protoplasm into the human race, has brought
forth, in so doing, a higher and altogether novel kind of being capable of compassion, wonder, beauty, and truth, although each form is
as precious, as sacred, as the other. The interdependence of everything with everything else in the totality of being includes a participation of nature in history and demands a participation of the
universe.

The future brings us nothing, gives us nothing; it is we who in
order to build it have to give it everything, our very life. But to be
able to give, one has to possess; and we possess no other life, no

living sap, than the treasures stored up from the past and digested, assimilated, and created afresh by us. Like all human activities, the law of growth, of evolution, of convergence draws its vigor from a tradition which does not die.

At this point, however, we must remember that the law of growth, of evolution, has both a creative and a tragic nature. This we recognize as a degenerative process, as devolution. Whether it is the growth of a human soul or the growth of a living cell or of the universe, we are confronted not only with fulfillment but with sacrifice, with increase and decrease, with enrichment and diminution. Choice and decision are necessary for growth and each choice, each decision, excludes certain potentialities, certain potential realities. But since these unactualized realities are part of us, they possess a right and command of their own. They must avenge themselves for their exclusion from existence. They may perish and with them all the potential powers of their existence, their creativity. Or they may not perish but remain unquickened within us, repressed, lurking, ominous, swift to invade in some disguised form our life process, not as a dynamic, creative, converging power, but as a necrotic, pathological force. If the diminishing and the predatory processes comingle, atrophy and even death in every category of life ensue. But if we possess the maturity and the wisdom to accept the necessity of choice, of decision, of order and hierarchy, the inalienable right of freedom and autonomy, then, in spite of its tragedy, its exclusiveness, the law of growth endows us with greatness and a new moral dimension.

Convergence is committed to the search for the deeper meanings of science, philosophy, law, morality, history, and technology—in fact all the disciplines in a transdisciplinary frame of reference. This series aims to expose the error in that form of science which creates an unreconcilable dichotomy between the observer and the participant, thereby destroying the uniqueness of each discipline by neutralizing it. For in the end we would know everything but *understand nothing*, not being motivated by concern for any question. This series further aims to examine relentlessly the ultimate premises on which work in the respective fields of knowledge rests and to break through from these into the universal principles which are the very basis of all specialist information. More concretely, there are issues which wait to be examined in relation to, for example, the philosophical and moral meanings of the models of modern physics, the question of the purely physicochemical processes versus the postulate of the irreducibility of life in biology. For there is a basic correlation of elements in nature, of which man is a part, which cannot be separated, which compose each other, which converge, and alter each other mutually.

Certain mysteries are now known to us; the mystery, in part, of the universe and the mystery of the mind have been in a sense revealed out of the heart of darkness. Mind and matter, mind and brain, have converged; space, time, and motion are reconciled; man, consciousness, and the universe are reunited since the atom in a star is the same as the atom in man. We are homeward bound because we have accepted our convergence with the cosmos. We have reconciled observer and participant. For at last we know that time and space are modes by which we think, but not conditions in which we live and have our being. Religion and science meld; reason and feeling merge in mutual respect for each other, nourishing each other, deepening, quickening, and enriching our experiences of the life process. We have heeded the haunting voice in the Whirlwind.

The Möbius Strip

The symbol found on the cover of each volume in Convergence is the visual image of *convergence*—the subject of this series. It is a mathematical mystery deriving its name from Augustus Möbius, a German mathematician who lived from 1790 to 1868. The topological problem still remains unsolved mathematically.

The Möbius Strip has only one continuous surface, in contrast to a cylindrical strip, which has two surfaces—the inside and the outside. An examination will reveal that the Strip, having one continuous edge, produces *one* ring, twice the circumference of the original Strip with one half of a twist in it, which eventually *converges within itself*.

Since the middle of the last century, mathematicians have increasingly refused to accept a "solution" to a mathematical problem as "obviously true," for the "solution" often then becomes the problem. For example, it is certainly obvious that every piece of paper has two sides in the sense that an insect crawling on one side could not reach the other side without passing around an edge or boring a hole through the paper. Obvious—but false!

The Möbius Strip, in fact, presents only one monodimensional, continuous ring having no inside, no outside, no beginning, no end. Converging with itself it symbolizes the structural kinship, the intimate relationship between subject and object, matter and energy, demonstrating the error of any attempt to bifurcate the observer and participant, the universe and man, into two or more systems of reality. All, all is unity.

I am indebted to Fay Zetlin, artist-in-residence at Old Dominion University in Virginia, who sensed the principle of convergence, of emergent transcendence, in the analogue of the Möbius Strip. This symbol may be said to crystallize my own continuing and expanding explorations into the unitary structure of all reality. Fay Zetlin's drawing of the Möbius Strip constitutes the visual image of this effort to emphasize the experience of convergence.

R.N.A.

WHO MADE YOU?

1   In Search of Truth and Faith

This inquiry is introduced by William Blake's haunting poem *The Tyger*. The entire poem is given for the convenience of the reader as note 1, at the end of the chapter.[1] The lines which challenge inquiry are:

> Tyger! Tyger! burning bright
> In the forest of the night . . .
> Did he who made the Lamb make thee?

There is a new answer to that question, one that William Blake could not possibly have formulated and that has profound implications for mankind today and tomorrow. The answer may be found partly in old texts reread in new light—new light provided by the multitude of scientific advances which are constantly expanding our frontiers of knowledge and providing new perspectives for understanding with respect to the physical universe around us, and therefore with respect to our own role in it. This explosion of scientific knowledge has occurred in a great variety of disciplines, as far apart as astrophysics and microbiology, all of which has implications for the arts and social sciences.

In particular, the present perhaps venturesome, hopefully evocative inquiry into our perceptions of "God" and "truth" has been touched off by a historian's[2] understandable bewilderment and distress over the atrocities which man has committed against man since history began—and is continuing to commit—quite often invoking his God in the process. Fighting and terrorism in the Middle East, events in the Sudan and Ethiopia, in Southeast Asia, in Central America, and, to bring matters to our own doorsteps, violent crime in New York City and in other great cities or even small towns in every part of the world, challenge our professed belief in a just and kindly God. Not only that! They affect our life-style now and threaten our existence in the future. It is a practical question; can men learn to live together in peace and harmony? Can they survive?

The particular aspect of this challenge addressed in this paper has to do with re-examination of the widely held assumption that there is an all-wise and all-powerful God somewhere "up there" who has told us what we should be doing to achieve peace and harmony which we would achieve if we would only do it. Theologians study God and tell us what He wants us to do; theocrats try to make us do what He allegedly has said.

Such is the fundamentalists' premise, certainly in Judaism, Christianity, and Islam, religions based on "revelation." These three closely related families of religion now embrace two-thirds of the populations living on our planet insofar as religious affiliations are known. The trouble seems to be that God has told different people different things, and a good deal of the bloodshed which stains the pages of history or which is happening today seems directly attributable to people who profess to be acting in accordance with God's truths as revealed to them.

We shall examine revealed truth with considerable skepticism. It seems self-evident that, regardless of how perfect the source of revelation, the process of receiving and transmitting it to fellow human beings (the role of the prophet) necessarily involves human beings and therefore the possibility of error. Different prophets have received quite different revelations—some simply irreconcilable with others. Even the same prophet may receive different, conflicting revelations at different times. Muhammad was a case in point. When challenged he responded in effect that he transmitted whatever message Allah chose to send down. Allah was all-knowing, all-wise, and all-powerful. What He thought good for people to know at one time might be different from what was good at another. He had the power to change his mind if He willed to do so.

And again, regardless of what the real nature of God may be, it is abundantly evident that human perceptions of that nature differ widely among different people at different times and places. Our conclusion will be that human beings are indeed in the presence of a vast universal power and are uniquely endowed with both the capability and the compulsion to relate to that power. It is, however, a capability and compulsion that arises out of the quality of being human—variable and fallible, not absolute or infallible. Cosmologies constructed on the basis of "divine" revelations of the distant past postulating "truths"—sacrosanct, immutable and eternal—simply fall apart.

At first we stand aghast amidst the rubble. Then we realize that we are alive, well, and very much part of exactly the same "eternal" scheme of things, which human beings have been looking at since they emerged onto the cosmic stage through the evolution process. Perceptions that were formulated during the early childhood of human intellectual evolution (anywhere from 1,500 to 3,000 years ago, or longer) are in need of update. Now we look at the same stars and the same hills and much the same sort of people with the same reverence and affection, but our perception is new.

This is not just an individual experience, but the common experience of all humankind as it passes out of cultural and intellectual childhood into what one may call the "scientific era." It is the same old universe, perhaps 15–20 billions of years old, the same old Earth,[3] which has been supporting life for perhaps 4–6 billion years, now seen as vibrant with an energy that is always new and yet as old as the universe or older—perhaps the only entity to which we can refer as truly eternal.

What is new and extraordinary about it is *us*—humankind—now perceived as the product of a process that began with the big bang 15–20 billion years ago, a process which took on a totally new dimension with the synthesis of life here on Earth 4–6 billion years ago, and which finally, through random genetic mutations, developed us as the first creatures ever gifted with certain special physical and mental characteristics, including we believe, genetically innate spiritual leanings. These mark us as being different from (and on balance superior to) other animal forms.

This latter event (the appearance of Hominids) occurred extremely recently in terms of cosmic time: only perhaps 2 million or so years ago. Very much more recently a creature emerged who could be called modern man, using Cro-Magnon man (35,000 or so years ago) as the milestone representative of that advance. "Civilization" (never adequately defined) may be said to have made its debut about 12,000 years ago. The foundations of our religious beliefs seem even more recent. Moses lived only about 3,200 years ago, Christ 2,000 years ago and Muhammad 1,400 years ago. There were earlier religious expressions, and shamanist cults still survive. Modern science was born perhaps 400 years ago. Darwin's watershed publications (watershed in the sense that the minds of the thinking public were awakened in a way that could never be reversed) appeared a little over 100 years ago, the big bang theory about 50 years ago. The pace of new discoveries seems to grow faster and faster.

William Blake, who asked that very pregnant question, "Did he who made the Lamb make thee?," died when Darwin was 16 years old. The simple but devout religious beliefs expressed in Blake's poetry and art do not suggest that the tyger and the Lamb were intended to present any deep allegory relating to human nature. However, such a reading would be valid under the more complex understandings of who we are and how we got here, introduced by the works of Darwin, Hubble, Lemaître, Hawking, Pagels, and of other modern researchers in the physical—and social—sciences.

It is a layman's inquiry inviting thoughtful consideration by other laymen, and constructive criticism by those professionally better qualified to speak about the scientific aspect. It is, as suggested above, a historian's search for some rational explanation of human savagery toward fellow beings, not in naive hope of finding a formula for universal peace and harmony among all people everywhere, but with the practical aim of removing some cherished misconceptions and illusions that certainly have exacerbated—and in some cases provided the sole cause of—wars, persecutions, and other inhumane behavior.

It is the mission of a historian to find out what *really* happened, and to tell it like it really was. The same challenge, of course, faces all investigators in every field. It is the essence of research and advancement of understanding in all physical and social sciences. For the dedicated few this challenge becomes a pattern of mind and a way of life. In a less demanding or less intense way it infects everyone—whether world watcher or sports fan—who follows current events in the daily paper or in other media.

For a historian, the greatest excitement is provided by new archaeological discoveries or the recovery of unknown documents (the Dead Sea Scrolls, for example), which open up new untrodden fields for original research. However, some small kind word may be said for the historian who braves well-known fields in which sacred cows have long been pastured, some of which can be shown to be diseased and in dire need of veterinary services, others dead giving rise to need for carcass removal.

For the sake of clarity and emphasis, the last-named type of historian's role may be compared with that of the small boy in Hans Christian Andersen's delightful fairy tale about the emperor's clothes. You remember the story:

Some very clever weavers presented themselves at court and represented to the emperor that they could weave the most beautiful cloth which had ever been seen on Earth, and it would have the magic property of being visible only to virtuous people, the sort of people over whom he ruled, but invisible to dishonest, sinful people. He sent his ministers to investigate, and they reported that it was indeed the most beautiful cloth in the world. Accordingly the weavers were commissioned to go ahead. They carried off this hoax in great style—paragons of charismatic showmanship. Finally the great day came. The emperor was robed in his magic garment, to the great admiration and acclaim of all the ministers of state. He went forth to show off his new clothes to the populace. There too he received the plaudits of the crowds—until a little boy was heard to say, "But Mommy, he doesn't have any clothes on!" Then they all saw.

As point of departure in our inquiry, we may make use of a slight misquote from Nietzsche's *Der Antichrist*:[4] "faith is belief in the untrue." Nietzsche was the son of a clergyman. He was writing of the Christian theological establishment of his time, but alas the real target of his attack seems not to have been so much the "faith" manifested in a blind acceptance of outworn myth or a pharisaical insistence on doctrines, creeds, dogma, ritual requirements, and other theological controls that it imposed, but rather a "faith" that glorified the sick and downtrodden, the outcast and disreputable. At that time, a generation after Darwin's publications, progressive thinkers were already questioning and discrediting much of the material supporting this doctrinal "faith."

Nietzsche also was not attacking the church's bureaucratic structure. The latter, though a worldly necessity, inevitably confutes and discredits the idealistic intent of the religion's founder. He was not attacking the low quality and occasional venality of the clergy/priesthood, nor their encouragement of ignorance, superstition, and prejudice, nor their occasional misuse of political influence. His attack appears as an attack of the *übermench* on a "faith" that protected and even glorified the poor and oppressed, the lonely, the helpless, those sick, or in prison (however justly they may have been placed there), and those suffering from a sense of sin, or from physical hunger. Historically, church establishments have often fallen far short of their mission in actual ministry to the needy and oppressed, but that mission does exist.

We shall assume that Nietzsche had read Darwin and had found the survival of the fittest concept all too compatible with the position he held as exponent of the *übermench*. By definition *übermench were* the fittest. Thus the Christian church, with its protection and even glorification of the "unfit" was, to Nietzsche, obstructionist in practice and retrogressive in principle. We all obviously repudiate any such position. Nevertheless Nietzsche's statement by itself is provocative; much that is accepted on the basis of religious faith *is* literally untrue: contrary to physical reality, contrary to common sense—sometimes intentionally so.[5]

Faith is a complex word, and there can be several different understandings depending on context. Illustrative of that point, the *Oxford English Dictionary* identifies 14 different definitions for the word "faith," classified into four major subdivisions—a degree of refinement that the average reader will not care to pursue. Three categories of meaning will suffice for the limited usage contemplated in this work:

1. "Dead" faith, represented by required assertions (creeds, oaths of allegiance, and similar declarations) imposed by a church or any other institution as a condition of membership. Those assertions are often accepted and repeated mechanically without any real thought or personal conviction, but they do represent a potent and sometimes injurious form of thought control.

2. "Live" faith, which is personal to the individual, a part of his or her psyche—a personal "cosmology," which can be a major factor in the individual's spiritual well-being, mental health, and adjustment to the environment. Whether the individual's own beliefs, which form the basis of this type of faith, are entirely rational is of secondary importance as long as they make sense for the individual, have no serious negative

effects on associates and loved ones, and do not create a hazard for the public at large.

3. "Working hypothesis" faith, represented by, for example, Columbus setting out for India by sailing west, or a scientist working out some research project, solidly convinced as to where it will lead, but not as yet able to demonstrate the validity of that conviction. This kind of faith provides a sort of psychic guidance for the researcher's project. If continuing research does not support his "faith," he will return to the point from which he started, disappointed perhaps but not defeated, able to establish and pursue a new line of reasoning with new faith in the outcome.

We will do well to illustrate these variations of faith with a few examples. The most dramatic and devastating examples are the many religious persecutions that have been carried out to preserve "the purity of the faith" or to enforce obedience. This of course would illustrate category 1 above.

The Roman Empire, starting with the Emperor Augustus (27 B.C.–A.D. 14) initiated the practice of deifying the emperor. Under the very accommodating ground rules of the Greco-Roman religion this presented no problem. Great strength, good luck, beauty, wealth, or any other outstanding characteristics attributed to mythological heroes and heroines were usually explained by the belief that he or she had a god or goddess as one parent after union with a mortal. The Romans easily welcomed new deities to their pantheon, including gods taken over from the religions of the peoples they had conquered. (St. Paul reminds us that there was in Athens a temple to "the unknown god," a form of theological insurance to make sure they had not overlooked and thereby offended any of the innumerable gods and goddesses whom they conceived of as existing "out there.")

The reigning emperor was by definition such a man: a man of extraordinary strength and wisdom, or perhaps simply extraordinarily lucky (or unlucky, as it turned out rather frequently) to have been thrust into a position of such power and grandeur—in any case, a man set apart from other men. As a symbol of the state's power, he had a certain spiritual relationship to all the people, which was not too different from that of other gods. Each represented a special type of power that could be worshipped.

Despite remarkably wise and tolerant laws respecting the religions of all conquered peoples, and of the Jewish people in particular, the idea that all subjects of the Empire should perform an act of worship toward the head of state was deemed necessary for the unity and well-being of that vast and heterogeneous entity. The act of worship in this respect had about the same religious and political intensity as taking the oath of allegiance to the United States. The latter incidentally does, or used to, have a reference to God, and thereby managed to arouse the heated opposition of some religious activists.

This Roman requirement seems to have presented insuperable problems for devout Jews and Christians. When enforced, it led to the great waves of Christian martyrdoms, of which every Sunday-school attender has lurid memories. For the Jews of Palestine at that time, who were already bitterly resentful of Roman rule, it may have been the spark that touched off the two hopeless, suicidal revolts led by Zealots, in A.D. 66–70 and in A.D. 132–35. Both provoked ruthless retaliation. However, it was confined to Palestine, and therefore cannot be compared with Hitler's unprovoked genocidal holocaust during World War II. Jews elsewhere were not affected. There are reports of mob actions against colonies of Jews, in Alexandria for example, in which the Roman army was employed to protect the Jews.

The Roman Empire's persecutions of Christians are now seen as having had a purely political objective—political thought control perhaps but not religious thought control. The only feature of the Christian faith that Roman authorities cared about or understood was its (to them) irrational and therefore suspicious opposition to Emperor worship. The persecutions were an unfortunate and mistaken response to a mistaken signal. It is difficult to say to what extent they were exacerbated by pure sadism on the part of the persecutors.

Later, after Christianity had turned the scales by becoming the state religion, it in turn carried out extensive persecutions against its own heretical minorities, and also sporadically against other religions, particularly the Jews. The Roman Church's later persecutions against fellow Christians who held heretical views were ostensibly purely theological, though overtones of personal power struggles among the players are not wanting.[6]

The idea of maintaining the purity of the orthodox Roman Catholic faith by force, that is, by persecution, did not die easily. It can be seen again in the Albigensian Crusade of the thirteenth century. The Dominican order of monks, founded at that time ostensibly for the purpose of preaching the faith, was also principally responsible for enforcing it by other means, notably in the Spanish Inquisition, active from about 1492, and for the next century or longer. After the establishment of a separate and politically powerful Protestant Church in the sixteenth century, persecutions for faith can be traced to that source. All this may be laid to faith category 1.

Columbus, as we have noted, had faith that the Earth was round at a time when orthodox thinking held it to be flat. This provides us with an early example of our third category of faith, and his faith obviously led to an event of major historical importance.

An example of faith (type 1) acting as a barrier to human progress is as follows: Copernicus (1473–1543) developed the idea that our sun, not Earth, was the center of the universe as it was known at that time. (Distant stars apparently had not come within reach of the instruments then available.) Copernicus's work was probably completed about 1530, but because of fear of unpleasant confrontation with the "defenders of the faith," or for whatever reason, it was not published until the year of his death. In a delayed reaction, the Curia in 1616 denounced the Copernican system as dangerous to the faith.

What probably brought it to their attention was its espousal by the distinguished and articulate astronomer, Galileo (1564–1642), who added many contributions of his own and attracted much interest in intellectual circles. Galileo was warned but continued his dangerous path. In 1633 he was tried by Papal Inquisition (separate and apart from the Spanish Inquisition) and ordered to publicly abjure his belief that our sun was the central body while Earth and the other planets moved around it. According to tradition, he rose from his knees after the abjuration muttering: "Nevertheless it does move." Presumably the Papal Curia has dropped its insistence that Earth is the center of the universe (and Rome the center of the Earth), but so far as this writer is aware, the condemnation of Galileo has not been rescinded.

Our second category of faith is perhaps more important to more people than the first: personal faith, in contradistinction to official or public faith. Personal faith does not make history.

The proposition that faith is belief in the untrue carries an implied challenge to substitute truth for untruth. One cannot—and would not wish to if one could—examine all the widely different individual formulations of belief that make up personal faith. There would be as many variations, nearly, as there are people, even among people who subscribe publicly to some one of the recognized unified faiths: Jewish, Christian, Islamic, Buddhist, Hindu, or other. Private faith, whether based on truth or nonsense, becomes a public concern only when it affects other people. Belief in a future life is usually a private matter; yet when a devotee of the strange medieval sect called Assassins (or a modern Muslim car-bomb terrorist) becomes convinced that the murder of a person represented to him as an unbeliever (an act that will inevitably involve his own death) assures him of eternal bliss in paradise—then private faith becomes a public concern.

Most examples are not so dramatic. The stubborn and pervasive belief within Judaism—which is indeed one of the pillars of Judaism—that God chose Abraham and gave him that name instead of Abram because of his virtue, assured him of His special care, and promised that this "specialness" would pass by heredity to his progeny through Sarah (later limited to the 12 sons of Jacob/Israel and to their descendants forever, as long as they kept a certain covenant)—has been for the Jewish people an enormously effective personal bulwark against the agonies of rejection, adversity, and dispersion. The salutary value of this particular article of faith (whether God actually said it to Abraham or some later scribe inserted it in the record as a pious invention) as a source of inner strength to the individual who holds it, must be weighed against the observation that, collectively, it has been an important factor in causing the very rejections and adversities—the "anti-Semitism"—against which it is so effective a bulwark.

One should note in passing the historical fact that dispersion of the Jewish people was not "punishment." To be sure, the ten northern tribes, who had broken off and formed a separate kingdom after the death of Solomon (ca. 933 B.C.), were conquered by the Assyrians after about two centuries of independence; the people were dispersed and their ethnic identity lost. That area was colonized by Samaritans, who may or may not have been related to these lost tribes. Not long after, the southern kingdom was also conquered, and its inhabitants carried off in 586 B.C. to Babylon. It is not clear what numbers of people were carried off, either in absolute numbers or as a percentage of the Jewish population residing at that time in Palestine. It probably did include all the religious and intellectual elite, but certainly not all Jews. The people who went to Babylon learned much while there, and greatly enriched the body of material that was eventually collected into what we know as the Old Testament. When the option to return was opened in 538, only a limited number of the Jews in captivity, chiefly the zealots and hotheads among them, chose to return to Palestine. Many chose to remain in Babylon, including the weightier religious leaders. Babylon—later Baghdad—remained the intellectual capital of Judaism for well over 1,000 years, until about A.D. 1200, the time of Maimonides.

Beginning before this compulsory diaspora and continuing after the return to Jerusalem in 538 B.C., colonies of Jews emigrating from Palestine settled voluntarily in the principal commercial centers of the Roman Empire, living together in their own quarter and maintaining their religious identity. In the first century A.D., Jewish people constituted probably 10 percent of the population of the Roman Empire, according to an estimate by Philo of Alexandria (order of magnitude: 6 million out of 60 million). Well over half probably lived outside of Palestine. These estimated numbers do not include any of the Jews living in Babylon (then part of the parthian empire) nor other cities of the Middle East.

Jews living as minorities in their quarters in the various cities of the Roman Empire were in general subject to Roman law but received special treatment in recognition of their religious beliefs, and on occasion were, as we have noted, protected by Roman troops when local mobs threatened to overwhelm them. An important colony lived in Rome. We have glimpses from time to time of individual Jews who enjoyed favor and/or exercised influence with the emperor.

Only in Palestine were the Jews notably unruly; one might say virtually unrulable. Christ tried unsuccessfully to provide them with an independent *religious* kingdom, a kingdom of the mind, the Kingdom of Heaven, to be found within their own hearts here on Earth (as well as in the mansions of the heavenly father after death). That belief would have technically satisfied the promise of an "independent" kingdom in the Land of Canaan spoken of by the prophets and by biblical tradition. It would have been compatible and even symbiotic with the kingdom of Caesar or his local representative.

The Palestine of Christ's day was seething with irredentist (Jewish national) fervor. A heavenly kingdom could not satisfy the dream of worldly independence. An earlier uprising had been quelled, but individuals, members of the Zealot sect, and others (freedom fighters or terrorists, according to one's point of view) hid along roads in the mountains and did what they could to disrupt or embarrass Roman rule. They were national heroes (or martyrs when they were caught). One theory holds that Bar-Abbas, whom the people selected for pardon rather than Jesus when Pilate offered them release of one condemned prisoner in honor of their high holy day, was such a person—not a common murderer and thief, but one who had committed those crimes as a freedom fighter in the conviction that he would somehow serve the cause of Jewish independence, a national hero condemned to become martyr.

The "Jewish War," so fully documented by Josephus (66–70), and the uprising led by Bar-Kokba (132–35) were incidents in this blind pursuit of political independence. The Jewish population of Palestine was thereby indeed greatly depleted, partly by bloodshed in battle and mass executions of captives, partly by disease and starvation under siege conditions, and partly by enslavement and deportation of survivors. An extensive area around Jerusalem was cleared of all Jewish persons and for centuries after was kept clear. Nevertheless, considerable numbers of Jews did survive, and apparently lived as farmers or herdsmen in the hills of Judea.

Meanwhile, as we have noted, the Jewish colonies in cities in other parts of the empire lived on in peace, and went about their business under the protection of Roman law and Roman armies. History does record instances of Zealots who fled from·Palestine and were given hospitable shelter by Jewish colonies in the West. They tried to stir up trouble, but there is no record of any instance of their having received favorable hearing by any Jewish colonies in the West. Jewish uprisings elsewhere against Rome simply did not occur, nor was there any official retaliation against Jews elsewhere because their coreligionists had behaved so badly in Palestine.

The uprisings in Palestine seem to have been a sort of spontaneous combustion identified with the traditional faith of Judaism. Yet the actual excesses there seem rather to have been the work of a small activist minority called Zealots, whose religious fervor overcame the wiser and more realistic counsel of the cautious and conciliatory elements within the Jewish nation. In this interpretation, it was the faith that the individuals had formulated within their own minds rather than the institutional thought-control type of faith, which brought about all this senseless, unnecessary, and in the end futile suffering and bloodshed. Corporate faith (Judaism) had set the stage and provided the libretto for personal faith (Zealotry). It was a case of "live" faith (our category 2) creating a lethal hazard for the public at large.

This brings us back close to the point from which we departed. Faith *is* belief in things beyond human knowledge—often but not always untrue. To have faith is a necessary and desirable condition of human existence. Personal faith is the basic element in happiness, serenity, or, in medical terms, mental health. Whether or not the particular elements in a personal faith are true or untrue is of little or no importance to the historian or to the social scientist as long as there is an affirmative answer to the question: "Can other people live with them?"

In the best of all worlds, repressive thought-control types of faith—arising out of and dependent on ignorance, superstition, prejudice, and characterized by bigotry and hypocrisy—would give way to progressive, thought-leadership types of faith compatible with rapidly progressing modern scientific understandings as to what we humans really are.

And this leads us back to William Blake's question: "Did he who made the Lamb make thee (tyger)?" It is quite clear that "the Lamb" (note capital letter) meant, symbolically, Jesus of Nazareth, whom Blake regarded as the epitome of all that is beautiful and good in the human psyche, the perfect manifestation of the Holy Spirit or Logos guiding a human being (or as the Bible puts it, spirit made flesh). The tyger, on the other hand, would be the symbol and epitome of brute power or ruthless terror.

One can hardly imagine that Blake ever, even for a moment, entertained the idea that there might be two different creators, two Gods, one for the Lamb and one for the tyger. Therefore, his question should be taken as purely rhetorical and may be understood in the phrase "how amazing!" The real question is whether Blake was thinking literally about the feline carnivores of India and Siberia, predominantly nocturnal in real life (and hence presented poetically as "burning bright in the forests of the night"), or metaphorically about the brutal and ruthless rapacity in man's nature. And, if one metaphor, then possibly another? Forests of the night may be equated with ignorance, superstition, and prejudice among men—a suitable environment for metaphorical tygers in the form of government dictatorship and theocracy?

The ecologist, environmentalist, and zoologist also will interest themselves in the imagery of this poem. They may find it unfortunate that Jesus of Nazareth, certainly (to Christians, at least) one of the strongest of the great figures in history, should be symbolized by the lamb, a particularly stupid and helpless little creature, natural prey for the likes of tyger. Christ is not himself the lamb, but the shepherd—one who cares for the likes of the lamb.

They will find it ironic that the need to provide pasture for sheep and other domestic animals and crops useful for man's comfort and economic exploitation, has led to massive deforestation whereby the natural habitats of the noble tyger (and of very many other wild animals) are rapidly disappearing. Under pressures of human expansion, in real life, the tyger has become an endangered species, while lambs are multiplying abundantly. Following Blake's metaphor, however (or, more correctly, our metaphor inferred from Blake's poem), the tyger is flourishing and the lamb is endangered.

NOTES

1. Reference is to the poem by William Blake (1757–1827), reading in full as follows:

> Tyger! Tyger! burning bright
> In the forests of the night,
> What immortal hand or eye
> Could frame thy fearful symmetry?
>
> In what distant deeps or skies
> Burnt the fire of thine eyes?
> On what wings dare he aspire?
> What the hand dare seize the fire?
>
> And what shoulder, and what art,
> Could twist the sinews of thy heart?
> And when thy heart began to beat,
> What dread hand? and what dread feet?

What the hammer? What the chain?
In what furnace was thy brain?
What the anvil? What dread grasp
Dare its deadly terrors clasp?

When the stars threw down their spears
And watered heaven with their tears,
Did he smile his work to see?
Did he who made the Lamb make thee?

Tyger! Tyger! burning bright
In the forests of the night,
What immortal hand or eye
Dare frame thy fearful symmetry?

2. The alumni magazine of an ivy league college (whose football mascot and presumed role model happens to be the subject of Blake's poem reproduced above) not long ago carried a "Letter to the Editor" deploring the decline in literary elegance in general, and the editor's laxity in performing his duties in particular, because he had permitted the use of "a" rather than "an" before the word "historian." The editor simply said (rather lamely, we thought) that it was house policy to follow the author's manuscript except in case of obvious error. That however simply confirmed the correspondent's point about loss of elegance. Had the editor had time, or had the point been important enough, he might have quoted H. S. Fowler's *A Dictionary of Modern English Usage* (Oxford University Press): ". . . *an* was formerly usual before an unaccented syllable beginning with **h** (*an historical work*), but now that the **h** in such words is pronounced the distinction has become pedantic, and *a historical* should be said and written. . . ."

3. The prevailing convention of spelling the name of our unique planet with a lower-case "e" should be reexamined. The Earth is, after all, a place name just as much as New York or London. Even cosmic place names are, so far as one can determine always—with the single exception of "sun"— dignified with capitals for their initial letters: for example, Mercury, Mars, Venus, etc. (planets in our solar system); Arcturus, Deneb, Vega, etc. (stars); Capricorn, Cygnus, Lyra, etc. (constellations); and Andromeda, Milky Way, etc. (galaxies). Lower case "e" should be reserved for the crumbly material in which one can dig, or plow, or which one can pick up with one's hands. However, even though all other cosmic place names were to carry lower-case initials, our Earth still should be capitalized, as being the only astral body anywhere (so far as one can be sure) that supports life, including that very special unique form of life, modern man.

4. What Friedrich Nietzsche (1844–1900) actually said in his *Der Anti-*

christ, speaking of his bête noire, Christianity, is as follows: ". . . it is a matter of complete indifference whether something is true, while it is of utmost importance whether it is believed to be true. Truth and the faith that something is true: two completely separate realms of interest—almost diametrically opposite realms—they are reached by utterly different paths" (Section 23, Walter Kaufman translation) and "Faith means not *wanting* to know" (Section 52, Kaufman translation). Numerous other passages in *Der Antichrist* carry messages to the same effect, but the actual words, "faith is belief in the untrue," do not occur in the Kaufman translation.

5. Many other quotations from earlier authorities affirm in almost identical terms that faith was belief in "untruth"—but with diametrically opposite intent from what appears to have been Nietzsche's intent. For example:

> Jesus answered them, "Have faith in God. I tell you this: if anyone says to this mountain, 'Be lifted from your place and hurled into the sea,' and has no inward doubts, but believes that what he says is happening, it will be done *for him*. I tell you, then, whatever you ask for in prayer, *believe that you have received in and it will be yours*."
>
> (Mark 11:23–24, New English translation; author's italics)

> And what is faith? Faith gives substance to our hopes, and makes us certain of realities we do not see.
>
> (Paul, *Letter to the Hebrews* 11:1)

> *Certum est, quia impossible est*. It is sure, because it is impossible.
>
> [Quintus Septimus Tertullian (ca. 160–230) *De Carne Christi*: pt. ii, ch. 5]

> *Ideo credendum quod incredible*. It is believable because unbelievable.
>
> [Robert Burton (1577–1640) *Anatomy of Melancholy*]

6. It will be convenient to take note here of the historic struggle to enforce unity and discipline within the geographically scattered and culturally diverse community of Christians during the first few centuries of our Christian era. It was a sort of battle royal among many different perceptions of "truth." Today all contestants probably seem to the modern, scientifically oriented observer almost equally far from any real truth. More importantly it was a struggle between those who would impose an authoritarian hierarchical organization upon the Church, understandably patterned in many respects along the lines established by the administration of the Roman Empire at that time, against those who would retain the personal

faith of all individual worshippers as ultimate authority, while recognizing, of course, the need for consensus within each congregational unit. Unity would be achieved by the latter through education and charismatic leadership under guidance and within restrictions provided by the Bible. The latter is suggestive of the town-meeting system of government, which currently prevails in some parts of rural New England, and is most clearly seen as the basis for government of Congregational and Quaker denominations.

Most readers, unless precommitted on doctrinal grounds to one position or another, instinctively side with the little fellow, with the loser, with democracy over autocracy, and so forth. On this basis our sympathy would go with some of the early church fathers who were proponents of, and may even have died as martyrs for, theological formulations equally or even more absurd than those that have become frozen into the orthodox faith. The merits of different theological formulations become tangled up with the personality struggles of those who espouse them. Their impact on the history of their times had no necessary connection with the merit of their underlying theology. It was the sort of contest in which right does not make might, or visa versa. The authoritarian hierarchical party emerged victorious and set the pattern for the influence of the institutional Christian Church on history from the later Roman Empire to our times.

As the Roman Empire had sent tens of thousands of Christians to martyrs' deaths over an issue that it regarded as essential to the maintenance of its authority, namely acknowledgment of the Emperor as supreme ruler by performing an act of worship as to a god, so the institutional Christian Church sent tens of thousands of "heretics" to martyrs' deaths over an issue that it in turn regarded as essential to the maintenance of its authority, namely unquestioning acceptance of official doctrines, dogma, and creeds.

The dimensions and implications of this struggle are developed thoughtfully by Elaine Pagels in her book *The Gnostic Gospels* (1979). There, and elsewhere, one may observe the use of an imposed "faith" as a psychological weapon. The very act by which one individual or group persuades or forces another individual or group to accept as true that which is manifestly untrue, or which the other believes to be untrue, gives the aggressor a special psychological, perhaps almost hypnotic, power over the victim of the aggression.

This latter point is charmingly dramatized in Shakespeare's comedy, *The Taming of the Shrew*, where (in Act IV, Scene V) Petruchio has so cowed the fractious Katharina that she responds to his outrageous contradictions about the source of the light shining down upon them with, "And be it moon, or sun, or what you please. And if you please to call it a rush-candle, henceforth I vow it shall be so for me."

2 Creation Myths versus What Really Happened

It is the historian's mission, mentioned in Chapter 1, to find out what *really happened* and tell it like it was. History began with the emergence of humans as thinking creatures only a relatively few thousands of years ago. The universe began, as one now can say with considerable certainty, some 15–20 billion years ago. What is a historian doing in a field that belongs professionally to the astrophysicists?

The answer is simple. Everybody is interested at a layman's level in so important an event as the creation of the universe, and fascinated to know that only within the last 50 years or so has science arrived at what seems to be a definitive explanation—one that, so far at least, fits in with all or most of the existing observations. One can expect new theories, some strikingly new and some merely refinements on what is now known. The important thing is that we now have a body of verifiable information in which we can have real faith (using the hypothetical scientific sense of that word). This supplants a sacrosanct mythology in which many people have lost faith. If still newer information comes along and requires some revisions in the details of our present understanding, this new kind of faith will easily adjust.

Beyond that, the historian is professionally interested in what people think, partly to relate that to what actions they take as a consequence of the thought, and partly to point out alternative ways for human beings to think about themselves and about their role in the cosmic scheme of things. Perhaps it is none of the historian's business, but everybody is (or should be) interested in improving human beings' life-styles, or simply in survival of the species.

When Blake wrote his poem asking how the creator of the Lamb could have made the tyger, he hardly had any question but that they both had been created by God, nor that all creation had happened within the six-day period mentioned in the biblical myth. He would have explained any findings that did not fit this pattern of belief quite simplistically, but it is doubtful whether any disturbing information along that line had come to his attention. The science of paleontology began with the work of Baron Cuvier (1769–1832), a contemporary of Blake. As previously mentioned, Darwin had not even begun his work. Charles Lyell (1797–1875), 40 years younger than Blake, did not publish his popular and influential *Principles of Geology* until 1830–33, shortly after Blake's death.

The historian's direct challenge is not so much to explain the creation of the universe itself, but rather to explain creation of the creation myths. The latter process surely began soon after human beings emerged from among the other animals as thinking creatures, endowed apparently from the beginning with a capacity and compulsion to ask questions, to create in their imaginations abstract beings and to endow them with powers that enabled people to answer their own questions to their own satisfaction at the time. These matters are therefore properly within the boundaries of history.

Curiosity in children is a quality that one notes (sometimes with delight and sometimes with exasperation) also in other young animals—in puppies and kittens especially because they are domestic animals readily observed. Students of wild animal behavior find similar characteristics in the young of many other species. Thus juvenile curiosity may be set down as a scientific fact, much more virulent in some species than others, and in some individuals within a species, than others. Most animals and many humans run out of curiosity as they reach adult life, but some humans go on into adult years asking the same questions more seriously: Who made the sun? the moon? the stars? the mountains? the sea? me? Why do I feel this way or that way? Why do I have dreams? Why do the caribou come along sometimes and not other times?

To provide answers to these and innumerable similar questions, it was necessary to assume the presence of a designer and maker of it all and some entity who was watching over people, affecting their lives by means of dreams, feelings, food supplies, and in many other ways. We are obviously most familiar with the system of answers that was gradually worked out and shaped into the more or less homogeneous religious system set forth in our Bible with its close cousin, the Quran. We are quite familiar also with the Greco-Roman and Norse systems, and aware of other systems followed elsewhere.

Evidence assembled by anthropologists and students of mythology[1] makes clear the fact that some sort of concept of God, whether monotheistic or polytheistic, or animistic, is worldwide and as existed from earliest times. It is manifested in primitive shamanic observances, some of which still survive in remote parts of frica, Australia, and New Guinea, and among some of the Inuit, erhaps elsewhere. It was manifest in the quite sophisticated but ow defunct religious systems of the ancient Egyptians, Babylonians, and some Mesoamericans, and is of course manifest in the till-active, Semitic revealed religious systems, and in Buddhism, Hinduism, Tao, Confucianism, and others. The concept of God is universal; its manifestations are as diverse as humankind is diverse.

The same may be said of creation myths. In all those with which we are familiar, man is the central figure. He was God's masterpiece, made in His own image[2], with whom God was allegedly well pleased at time of creation (though He seems to have had reason to regret His action later). In the biblical and quranic versions, the Earth itself and all the plants, animals, and (although this will provoke an argument) even women were created by God for man's[3] support and pleasure.

There are two versions of the biblical creation myth. In the first, man was created to rule all the animals; God created man and woman simultaneously (Genesis 1:27). In the second, even woman was created only as an afterthought, to be a partner to man (Genesis 2:21–23). The Quran has numerous references to Allah as creator of the Earth and heaven and all that lies between them. Man was created of a lump of clay (could not possibly have been made in the image of God because Allah had no likeness), but Allah set him above the angels and commanded the angels to bow down before him.[4] Other passages in the Quran make it clear that Allah intended women to be subservient to men, yet protected and properly provided for.

Obviously man was (in his own opinion) the most important figure in this primitive universe (there was no reason for him to think
otherwise). In the Judeo-Christian tradition, men believed that God
had made them in His own image, and under the circumstances,
that was probably the highest compliment they could have paid to
God.

Mental images of God formed by men on the basis of their varied
experiences changed and developed as time went on. Our Bible,
which was written by many different people over a period of more
than 1,000 years, reflects many such changes. We shall devote a
separate chapter later to that subject. The important point to be
emphasized here has already been made: the concept of God is
practically universal among men. We hold that it is a genetically
innate character trait in the species *Homo sapiens*, one of the distinguishing features that differentiates that species from others.
However, the mental images of God that appear in men's writings
and are made manifest in their actions reveal an astonishing variation
in men's perceptions of that entity.

Thus, one must examine each proposition that has been set forth
as Word of God in the knowledge that it was written or said by a
human being somewhere, sometime, and must inevitably have been
conditioned by the personal views, prejudices, interests, experiences, and capabilities of that individual: the transmitters of the
Word, the "media" of those times.

To say, and demonstrate with convincing evidence, that a proposition transmitted to us as the Word of God (and held to be sacrosanct on the strength of that representation) is just plain wrong, is
not to repudiate the concept of God; it does call into question the
authority of men who claim to speak for God, but mostly it merely
says that modern science is a better question answerer than pious
intuition.

Everyone except the most fundamental of fundamentalists knows
that the world was *not* made in six days. Biblical creation stories
remain, and may be cherished as myths or allegory. For thousands
of years they answered people's questions about how they got here
(God made them), who they were (cherished protegées of God),
what they should do (obey his rules as revealed to Moses, et al.), and
so forth. Now we have a very different answer to the question of
how people got here, and that answer has ramifications throughout

the generally accepted answers to the other questions. We shall try to take these step by step.

Three major scientific "revelations" have reshaped "thinking man's" cosmology. The quotation marks draw attention to nonconventional use of both terms: first, by substituting well-organized and carefully disciplined scientific observation and analysis for revelation based on the psychological phenomenon of religious experience, alias pious intuition; and second, by narrowing use of the verb "to think" from a generic one that has been applied to all of *Homo sapiens* to one that focuses on only a very small fraction of the total of humanity, namely, people who are able to evaluate dispassionately and form valid judgments regarding the world in which they live. Included hopefully in that number of people would be the world leaders of the future.

First, logically, is the scientist's "revelation" regarding the creation of the universe. We shall deal with that in the next chapter. Next, in terms of cosmic time—although first by half a century to catch the general public's attention and pave the way for a general reshaping of its ideas about the role of human beings in the cosmic scheme of things—is Darwin's theory of evolution. This follows in Chapter 4. The third scientific revelation, containing perhaps even more far-reaching implications for human beings' ideas about their role in the cosmic scheme of things, is the slowly unfolding (still in its early stages) scientific knowledge and understanding of the physiology of the human brain. Discussion of this follows in Chapter 5.

NOTES

1. Notable studies of mythology available to the students of these matters, include that of Sir James G. Frazer (1854–1941), *The Golden Bough*, published originally in two volumes in 1910, enlarged to 13 volumes in the third edition (1952), and since reedited and abridged into a single volume by T. H. Gaster, in 1959. Also the work of Joseph Campbell (1904–1986), *The Masks of God* (1964), and many other works. Also the pioneer collection of German folk talks, known as *Grimm's Fairy Tales* (1812–15), which first attracted popular attention to this subject. Other studies of mythology mentioned by *Columbia Encyclopedia* are: E. B. Taylor, *Primitive Culture* (2 vol., rev. ed. 1924); Otto Rank, *The Myth of the Birth of the Hero* (translated 1952); Gertrude Jobes, *Dictionary of Mythology, Folklore and Symbols* (2 vol. 1961); and Thomas Bullfinch, *Mythology* (2nd ed. 1970). One may add: P. A.

Munch, *Norse Mythology* (revised and translated, 1954); *New Larousse Encyclopedia of Mythology* (translated, new ed., 1965); and Robert Graves, *The White Goddess* (1947) and *Greek Myths* (1956).

2. Some Voltairesque wit long ago observed: "In the beginning God created man in his own image, and man has been returning the compliment ever since." This or a similar remark has been attributed to Napoleon, but the attribution cannot be confirmed. What Voltaire himself (1694–1778) actually said is: "If God did not exist, it would be necessary to invent him" (*Epîtres*, xcvi, *à l'Auteur du Livre des Trois Imposteurs*).

3. In this instance only, and nowhere else in this paper, the term "man" is strictly limited to the male animal; elsewhere it always carries the meaning of mankind or humankind or people, terms in which womankind is included (one might even say embraced) as coequal in every respect. It is hard to identify a point in the evolution of culture or civilization at which woman became fully accepted in man's philosophy/cosmology as a coequal member of the human race in every sense of the word. Obviously, even today that utopian point has not been reached by all humankind. It was *not* inherent in the intuitive revelations that came to the early prophets, but *is* inherent in the "revelations" that come through rational scientific observations.

4. Muhammad depicts Allah as commanding the angels to bow down before his new creation (man):

> When your Lord said to the angels: "I am placing on the Earth one that shall rule as my deputy," they replied: "Will You put there one that will do evil and shed blood, when we have for so long sung Your praises and sanctified Your name?"
>
> He said: "I know what you do not know."
>
> He taught Adam the names of all things and then set them before the angels, saying: "Tell Me the names of those, if what you say be true."
>
> "Glory to You," they replied, "we have no knowledge except that which You have given us. You alone are wise and all-knowing."
>
> Then said He to Adam: "Tell them their names." And when Adam had named them, He said: "Did I not tell you that I know the secrets of heaven and Earth, and all that you hide and all that you reveal?"
>
> And when We said to the angels: "Prostrate yourselves before Adam," they all prostrated themselves except Satan (Iblis), who in his pride refused and became an unbeliever.
>
> Sura 2, "The Cow," 30–35 (Dawood translation)

One notes in passing the importance here attached to man's ability to name things. In the second of the two biblical creation myths, God brought all the wild animals and all the birds of heaven to man to see what he would call them, and whatever the man called each living creature, that was its name (Genesis 2:19).

In one of the most recently assembled collections of primitive myths, the Finno-Ugric *Kalevala* (compiled 1835–49), the hero, Vainamoinen, sings down his adversary, Joukahainen, in a battle of magic, the principal feature of which is, to the casual reader at least, the ability to sing the names of more things. Knowledge is power!

It is interesting also to note in passing that the makers of at least some of these myths having to do with the very earliest relationships between man and his gods, sensed the possibility that the gods might actually live in fear of the powers of the man-creature whom they had created. A bit of this is present in the story of the Tower of Babel. The Lord came down to see the city and tower which mortal men had built, and he said, "Here they are, one people with a single language, and now they have started to do this; hencefoward nothing they have a mind to do will be beyond their reach. Come, let us go down there and confuse their speech . . . " (Genesis 11:5–7). There is a bit of the same in Greek mythology, especially in stories having to do with Prometheus, and with Pandora's box. In the quotation from the Quran given above, the angels warned Allah about this creature man, but He wouldn't listen; He knew what they did not know. Man was His deputy on Earth and they were commanded to bow before him.

In all of the examples given, the God of the Hebrews, the Olympian gods of Greece, and Allah are perceived as possessing an anthropomorphic brain—just like the human brain with its associated powers only much better and therefore more powerful. It is a fundamental premise of this work that the concept of gods with anthropomorphic brains is inherently fallacious and did not exist prior to the emergence of "thinking man" onto the cosmic stage—so very recently in terms of cosmic time. The human brain is made up of specialized molecules joined together into neurons, probably several trillions of them, activated by some combination of chemical and electrical means involving other specialized molecules formed into neurotransmitters and by inhibitors that exist within the central nervous system. No molecules, no brain!

3 The Scientists' Creation Story

The big bang theory of the beginning of our universe is now generally accepted among astrophysicists and others whose professional opinions would have weight in these matters. It postulates an unimaginably huge explosion of densely packed particles that form the components of the atoms that comprise matter. Credit for presenting the first paper outlining the theory is usually accorded to a Belgian astrophysicist, the Abbé Georges Edouard Lemaître (1894–1966).

Curiously, the recent book, *A Brief History of Time from the Big Bang to Black Holes* (1988), by the distinguished British theoretical physicist, Stephen W. Hawking,[1] does not mention Abbé Lemaître's name, although Hawking is quite generous and meticulous in giving full credit to other scientists who have made major contributions to human knowledge and understanding in this and related fields. Hawking credits Edwin Hubble with having made the landmark observation that led to the conclusion that all matter must have been in one place at one time 10 to 20 billion years ago. That observation was published in 1929; Lemaître's theory was published in 1933.[2]

It is a commentary on the changing currents within the mainstream of public opinion that announcement of this revolutionary theory, so much at variance with the biblical account of creation, and with its far-reaching implications regarding the nature of the Creator, caused hardly a stir within the same conservative religious circles that had raised such an uproar over Charles Darwin's *Origin of Species* (1859) and *Descent of Man* (1871). Discussion of the big bang theory was for many years largely confined to gatherings of scientists, and to learned papers in journals that do not reach the general public. In recent years the big bang theory itself has received more notice in the public media. However, even the most devoted amateur science watchers are so caught up in trying to understand and digest the many new revolutionary scientific breakthroughs that the big bang has become "just one of those things."[3]

We must be sure that everyone is talking and thinking about the same thing when using the word "universe," of course. As *The New Columbia Encyclopedia* puts it, the universe is "the totality of matter and energy in existence." A closely associated word would be "cosmos." The encyclopedia goes on to say that the study of the origin of the universe is known as *cosmogony*. The study of its structure and evolution is known as *cosmology*. All of these words must be used with care. The "universe" of the remote ancestors who framed the biblical creation myths was not that of the educated public today, and even today the word is frequently used to define a particular specialty, for example, the "universe" of sports writers or computer users or whatever. Also the term cosmology appears in some scientific writings as connoting a particular school of thought among astrophysicists to distinguish them from others who belong to a different school of thought. By common agreement among readers of this paper (it is hoped), "universe" will embrace the *totality* of matter and energy, and "cosmology" will connote an individual's perception and understanding regarding the entire universe, including the related metaphysics (i.e., not just one aspect of astrophysics) at any given time.

There are a number of books about the big bang, ranging, in Hawking's opinion, from the very good (Steven Weinberg's *The First Three Minutes*) to the very bad (not identified). A few years ago, Dr. Heinz R. Pagels, president of the New York Academy of Sciences spoke before a small audience of interested laymen, describing to them the principal features of the big bang itself and the subsequent evolution of the universe as we know it. He carefully avoided the word "creation," explaining that he himself had no certainty about what if anything had gone before. Then, at one point in his presentation, when talking about the formation of matter during the cooling off period following the bang, he interjected a sort of aside or footnote, which caught the ear of this listener as the most important "new-horizon opener" in the entire presentation. "After all," he said, "many scientists now feel that matter is nothing but organized energy." We shall concentrate on that idea.

Every schoolboy is aware that the building blocks of matter are molecules. Most schoolboys also know that the molecules themselves are made up of atoms. There was a time within the memory of people who are still alive today when it was generally thought that atoms represented the ultimate unit or subdivision of matter. Not so! It is now known that the atom itself is a complex entity comprised of a nucleus surrounded by orbiting electrons. The nucleus contains protons and neutrons, each containing three quarks of three different types held together by gluons. The protons carry a positive charge; the neutrons carry no charge; the orbiting electrons carry a negative charge.

Here at last we have arrived at the ultimate units of which matter is composed—or have we? It is not easy to find out. The inquiring reader who has had the good fortune to run across an article entitled "Particle Accelerators Test Cosmological Theory," written by David N. Schramm and Gary Steigman (1988), will have read that there are only 12 fundamental particles of matter; six are quarks, mentioned above, and the other six are leptons. Electrons are classified among the leptons. The reader is left with unsatisfied curiosity as to the number of these various types of particles that may exist within a single atom. It *is* a much more real and much more serious question than the medieval theological question as to how many angels could stand on the head of a pin (and people were willing to die over the latter question). The inquiring layman also notes that nonmaterial forces such as light, sound, and gravity are made up of particles. Some particles have mass and some have none.

Study of the composition and behavior of atoms and their component particles is of great interest to scientists in order to understand many other natural phenomena observed, not only in their own but also all disciplines from astrophysics to microbiology. It is of great interest to us for a somewhat different reason: we seek to understand better and to test a hypothesis that energy is the essence of the universe and, conversely, that the universe is, in essence, simply organized energy. Under this hypothesis, energy was the creative force, is the sustaining force, and will be eventually perhaps the force that causes it to collapse (called by scientists familiarly, the "big crunch") into a densely concentrated mass of particles similar perhaps to that state in which it existed at the moment of the big bang.

In hasty defense of the last part of this hypothesis, we point out that individual stars do burn out and collapse. This phenomenon is well known among astrophysicists and occasionally finds its way into the public media. The results can be "white dwarf" stars whose diameter may be only a few thousand miles but whose density is hundreds of tons per cubic inch. Because of their great density, they have the gravitational characteristics of very much larger bodies and continue in orbit around other bodies on that basis. Much less is known about the newly discovered "black holes." The most plausible working hypothesis holds that these also are collapsed stars but of a density so great and a magnetic/gravitational force so powerful, that photon particles (light emissions) cannot leave their surface. It is well known that gravitational forces can deflect particles of light, and this would be an extreme example of that phenomenon. However, modern ultrasensitive instruments are able to pick up other forms of energy emissions, and it is on the basis of these that the astrophysicists postulate a black hole.

If stars collapse, why not universes? The question has fascinating implications. It raises the specter of infinite time, with one universe following another. One would postulate big-bang-to-collapse cycles perhaps millions of trillions of years long from bang to collapse, but what is time? Energy apparently would not be lost, although its "organization" would be converted successively from dense mass to gigantic fireball to stars-planets-galaxy formation, and so on. But where did the energy come from in the first place? How does it "know" to organize itself into matter and to obey certain laws that make its behavior predictable (within boundaries which take into account the newly discovered Laws of Uncertainty and Chaos)?

Such questions are essentially religious in nature, not too different from those that haunted early human beings almost as soon as they had developed in the evolutionary process to the point of possessing a unique mind capable of formulating thoughts and asking these sorts of questions.

Human beings' intellectual progress, starting with the Cro-Magnon period perhaps 35,000 years ago, or with the "dawn of civilization" in Egypt, Mesopotania, India, and China (and perhaps also in

Mesoamerica) about 10,000 to 12,000 years ago, has produced different sorts of answers at different times. At first, philosophical speculation and pious intuition provided answers with which a person could live by accepting them on faith (but which became a sort of Procrustean bed in time—if one wasn't comfortable in it, Procrustes cut or stretched him to size!) Today scientific observation is replacing pious intuition as the authority for acceptable answers and Procrustes, in our society at least, has been largely overcome.

The nature of time is a side issue, but an important one to scientists and religiously curious laymen alike. Hawking starts with the confession that mathematicians can't deal with infinity. So, for him, time (often expressed as "space-time") began with "singularity" at the moment of the big bang and would end at the big crunch if and when matter returns to singularity. He and those who share his school of thought know nothing of what went before the big bang— if indeed anything did go before—and anyway, anything that might have happened would be irrelevant and of no importance. All theories generated by this school of thought are based on scientific observations of phenomena occurring *since* the big bang. Hence time begins there. The Roman Catholic Church has endorsed that view (though it has not yet exculpated Galileo, so far as we know).

Nevertheless, it stands to reason philosophically that the mass of material that was about to go bang must have gotten there somehow. Something *had* happened before the big bang. If not the collapse of a previous universe, then perhaps some sort of synthesis of inchoate energy into particles such as we have been discussing above? Might the bang itself have been an "implosion" of inchoate energy rather than an explosion of preexisting particles? Indeed, there was a proposal put forward in 1941 by Hermann Bondi, Thomas Gold, and Fred Hoyle that matter is being created to fill empty spaces between galaxies as they move apart—the steady state theory. This theory met many of the conditions actually observed but not all, and eventually had to be abandoned. Other theories proposed "little bangs," involving (one would suppose) sudden revival of collapsed stars, or something of the sort.

More central to our philosophical inquiry is the question of the survival of existing particles, the quarks and leptons. One tentative hypothesis would hold that each particle now in existence is the same particle with the same electric charge (plus or minus or neuter) that was in existence at the time of the big bang and, if the philosophers' proposal of some previous existence can be sustained, had been in existence throughout eternity before that. The fact that at one time a particular particle would be part of hardest granite, and at another time part of the most delicate tissue, at one time part of a young vigorously growing plant or animal, at another part of a dead and decaying corpse, at one time part of a living star, at another part of one that had collapsed, at one time part of an atom that had (for example) three electrons orbiting at a certain distance from the nucleus, at another time part of the same atom in which the number of electrons and/or their distances from the nucleus had changed, or even of a different atom; all of this would make no difference whatsoever in the identity and character of the individual particle.

The opposite hypothesis, which is suggested by Robert K. Adair, suggests the "annihilation" of the vast majority of particles by their corresponding antiparticles. Annihilation of particles is a thought-provoking and actually somewhat scary proposition to be factored into our newly emerging cosmology. Perhaps the word "annihilation" does not mean quite what it seems to mean. Perhaps the "annihilated" particles are simply removed from the game for the time being—like an ice-hockey player sent to the penalty box or a chessman that has been taken up. Be that as it may, Robert Adair, formerly chairman of the Physics Department at Yale University and now at Brookhaven National Laboratories, asks the following question as the opener in his article, "A Flaw in a Universal Mirror," (1988):

Why is there matter in the universe? If the approximate symmetry between matter and antimatter that has been observed were perfect, the universe would have been elegantly simple, but virtually empty of matter and of creatures made up of that matter who could contemplate that elegance. The existence of the universe as we know it comes from a flaw. . . .

It seem that, at a time somewhere before the first millionth of a second after the universe was born in the fiery ball known as the big bang, matter and antimatter probably existed in equal amounts. There were almost exactly equal numbers of particles and antiparticles, all in thermodynamic equilibrium under conditions of enormous pressure and temperature (i.e., particles with same mass but opposite electrical properties; the positron is the antiparticle of the electron, for example . . .). Then as the universe expanded and cooled, most of the particles found their corresponding antiparticles and the pairs annihilated each other. . . . But the symmetry was slightly flawed and an excess of about one in a billion protons and one in a billion electrons survived to form, in the fullness of time, galaxies, stars, planets and ourselves.

The concept of a universe empty of matter and therefore of people to think about it and to wonder how they got here, what they should be doing in order to conform with the rules of the game, and so forth, is indeed sobering, as is the suggestion that only one one-billionth part of the particles involved in the big bang survived to constitute the universe as we know it. That is still quite a lot of particles when one stops to think of all the uncountable billions of galaxies, stars, planets, and so on, and especially all of us human beings—all five billion of us now—struggling to find physical and spiritual fulfillment, to live in peace and harmony with each other, and (perhaps a more urgent point), simply to survive on this unique Earth. The latter, although a very rich planet indeed, does have limitations as to what it will support.

How did Earth get to be so rich? How did it happen to have all the elements necessary for life to be synthesized and for life to survive? Photographs sent back from interplanetary space probes make it probable that some of the conditions necessary for life (e.g., water in liquid state) were once present on some at least of the other planets in our solar system, but it is almost certain that no life does exist at the present time anywhere else within our solar system. As to other solar systems we have no scientific knowledge; science fiction has taken over!

It remains to examine in this chapter how Earth got so rich, and in the next how man came to exist. Certainly both Earth and man are unique, interdependently so.

It will not be especially helpful to this inquiry to attempt a digest of present scientific knowledge about the evolution of the universe or the geological endowment of the planet Earth. Two reasons for this are: (1) the information that amateur science watchers are able to acquire is sure to be incomplete and out of date; and (2) amateurs are very likely to get it at least partly mixed up or completely wrong! Suffice it to say that the intensely hot fireball created by the big bang (temperatures 4 trillion times hotter than normal room temperature) did expand and cool off. One may ask what happened to the heat but there is no immediate explanation.

At some point in the cooling process, particles formed into atoms,

atoms formed molecules, and the latter became elements. Isotopes of helium, hydrogen, lithium, and beryllium were formed at this time; other elements found in the atomic-weight chemical element tables, about which high-school students learn in chemistry class, apparently were formed later. Schramm and Steigman provide a timetable in graphic presentation of this formation period in their article about particle accelerators, mentioned above.

The layman sees this stage of the universe as a hodge-podge of particles, atoms, molecules, and bits of molten matter in process of agglomeration, all swirling about, looking for someone else with whom to become partners. Eventually solar systems and galaxies emerged from the melée. The latter were, of course, manifestations of the force of gravity counterbalanced by centrifugal forces and inertia acquired in the big bang.

There were also great numbers of unattached, or as one might say, "maverick" bodies, careening about, often colliding with each other and with established planets. This process had much to do with what elements ended up where.

Most of the "maverick" astral bodies eventually found permanent homes. A few apparently are still at large. Halley's Comet, and one nicknamed Nemesis apparently are of this type. They are being tracked and their future orbits studied by modern astronomers. The public is assured that they will not pose any threat to the Earth, at least not for 60 million years or so!

Our Earth, as one might have expected, experienced several major collisions of this type, plus innumerable smaller ones. Such happenings are credited with bringing to our planet a variety of elements, some of which would have been lacking after the first random assemblage of hot particles. Interestingly, one such collision, while the Earth was still in a semimolten state, is credited in one theory with depositing heavier elements and plopping lighter ones out just far enough to become our satellite, the Moon. Of greatest interest to us, naturally, is the resultant chance assemblage here of all elements necessary for the later synthesis of life.

The key questions for the layman are: (1) How did certain molecules end up on certain astral bodies; and (2) how were the additional chemical elements and their compounds eventually synthesized (not only how but where). There are no immediate answers to these questions.

However, these questions introduce a major factor in the evolution of the universe, which will also be a major factor in the evolution of life on Earth and in the evolution of man himself: random chance. Random chance is a difficult pill to swallow. Scientists resent it because they seek patterns of behavior that they can predict, and random chance seemingly disrupts the orderly rule of natural law (unless partially accounted for in some instances by Werner Heisenberg's Uncertainty Principle (1926) or the new science of Chaos, which has emerged only quite recently). If something can be accounted for by natural law, it is predictable; happenings by random chance are by definition not predictable. One knows that such happenings will "just happen" with great frequency but they are *not* predictable.

Church groups, on the other hand, reject or minimize the random-chance factor because they have chosen to see the hand and will of God in virtually all happenings. Many of the things that God "plans" and "does" (in accordance with this theory) may seem irrational and even cruel, but He knows, He has a plan, He moves in wondrous ways His wonders to perform and, for people who have faith, all will work out best in the end, in accordance with God's wisdom.

This belief that God has everything under control is central to Islam (the name means "submission"—patient unquestioning surrender to the will of God). It is also more or less implicit in Judaism and Christianity. As an article of faith, it can be a powerful comfort and support to the individual beset by adversity. Nothing said here should minimize that beneficent effect in the lives of those who possess faith that God is in His control tower, so to speak, watching over each individual, monitoring his or her flight plan, and keeping in touch by intercom.

However, this is not an article of faith that can be supported by scientific observation. Modern man with his remarkable brain (made up of molecules, be it noted) has the ability and proclivity to utilize natural law for his purposes and, under laboratory conditions, to conduct physical and chemical experiments, with minimum interference from random chance. It makes no sense, however, for people to project this ability (i.e., their own limited ability to arrange and plan) into their image of a (nonmolecular) spirit "out there," a disembodied spirit possessing a suprahuman anthropomorphic brain di-

recting the heavenly bodies in their courses, all in accordance with a
wise and careful plan whose first objective was the creation of
human beings, and then their well-being and comfort.

The Earth's original "draw" in terms of chemical elements, including matter capable of being synthesized into other elements, was
a matter apparently of pure random chance. The Earth also received
many more elements as a result of innumerable chance collisions
with other astral bodies. The judgment that the Earth was more
fortunate than other planets, certainly in our solar system and so far
as we know elsewhere, can only be supported by the observation
that there *is* life here and not, so far as we know, elsewhere. Other
factors beside possession of a supply of oxygen, carbon, water in
liquid state, calcium, and other elements essential to life, provided
by random chance, would include a climate, neither too cold nor too
hot and the incidence of some happening that would spark the chemical reaction combining whatever elements into viable living tissue.

We lay to one side the question whether some other form of life
could have been synthesized utilizing different elements and would
have been viable in different climatic conditions. That is purely
academic. We are what we are because a combination of natural law
and random chance worked it out that way.

At every step of this evolutionary process, one can observe matter
behaving in predictable ways in accordance with natural laws that
are known to science (or will become known in the course of future
research) but also the enormously important interference of random
chance setting the stage and providing unpredictable collisions, mutations, and other chance happenings.

Two basic facts emerge from this discussion of subatomic particles (which, as always, are open to exhaustive re-examination by
one's favorite astrophysicist) that are especially pertinent to our inquiry. The first is the fact of an electric charge, positive or negative
as the case may be, attached to a predominant number of these
subatomic particles, providing attraction between opposite polarities
and a repelling action between like polarities. This fact is the basis of
gravity, which is probably the most important of the forces at work
in the complex interrelationships of the heavenly bodies, but it has
many other important applications as well. One may venture (more
as a question than as a statement of fact) the thought that the dynamism imparted to matter at the moment of the big bang, and the

dynamism of the evolving universe ever since, are both dependent upon this principle.

The second basic fact grows out of the first. These subatomic particles remain in existence and retain their polarity (at least a sufficient number of them do, despite the apparent wholesale annihilation by antiparticles noted above) virtually forever, unaffected by almost any happening or condition to which they can be exposed. It does not seem to make any difference whether they are in a nuclear fireball or at temperatures close to absolute zero, or any of the other extremes suggested above. To be sure, the atoms of which they are part may be modified or changed under conditions of intense heat, or magnetic bombardment, which may happen in nature or be produced experimentally in particle accelerator apparatus, but the particles' individual integrity and basic polarity seems to remain unaffected.

With these facts in hand, we feel reassured in the hypothesis that energy *is* the essence of the universe, and vice versa. Of course, we are no nearer than before to understanding how these particles came into being in the first place, and/or how they get positive and negative polarities, and/or how they retain them all through cosmic time spans, if they do. Nevertheless, we are emboldened by the presumed fact that they do survive and do retain that polarity to suggest the further hypothesis that energy *is* eternal. That would depart somewhat from Professor Hawking's definition of space-time as beginning with the bang and ending with the crunch. It was in being before time began and will continue indefinitely even though all matter and the theories that go with it should be reduced once more to the state of "singularity" that existed just before the big bang.

NOTES

1. Stephen W. Hawking, *A Brief History of Time from the Big Bang to Black Holes* (New York: Bantam Books, 1988) (hereafter cited as *Brief History of Time*).

2. The following rather limited listing of source material regarding Lemaître and others who have written about the big bang was derived from the Columbia University Library's card catalog under the subject reference heading, "big bang":

- The big bang and Georges Lemaître: proceedings of a symposium in honor of G. Lemaître 50 years after his initiation of big bang cosmology (held at Louvania-Neuve, Belgium, 10–13 October 1983; edited by A. Berger; published by D. Reidel; and sold by Kluwer Academic publishers.

- Harold Fritzsch (1943–), *The Creation of Matter: The Universe from Beginning to End* (New York: Basic Books, 1984, translated from German).

- James S. Trefil (1938–), *The Moment of Creation: Big Bang Physics from Before the First Millisecond to the Present Universe.* (New York: Charles Scribner's Sons 1983).

Columbia Encyclopedia has a brief notice regarding Lemaître, as follows: "Lemaître, Georges, Abbé, 1894–1966, Belgian astrophysicist and mathematician. He postulated the theory that the universe originated as a condensed primeval atom that exploded, producing the force by which the universe is still expanding."

The same source (*Columbia Encyclopedia*) has the following notice regarding Hubble:

Hubble, Edwin Powell, 1889–1953, . . . He discovered that there are large-scale galaxies, or independent star systems, lying far beyond the Milky Way and that these galaxies are distributed almost uniformly in all directions. He was the first to offer observational evidence to support the expanding theory of the universe, presenting his findings in what is now known as HUBBLE'S LAW. . . .

The latter is subject of a longer article describing the principles involved in Hubble's Law, and subsequent work by others which has caused changes in some of the values postulated by Hubble. The date of Hubble's Law is 1929. Thus it pre-dated Lemaître's paper by about four years.

Steven Weinberg's work, *The First Three Minutes, a Modern View of the Origin of the Universe*, which Hawking praises as the best source of information about the big bang, was first published in 1977. An updated edition was published by Basic Books, New York, in 1988.

Closely related to the same interest is Heinz R. Pagels's *Perfect Symmetry, the Search for the Beginning of Time*, Bantam Books, New York, 1986. The latter is a reprint of the Simon & Schuster edition published in 1985.

All of the foregoing offer bibliographies or suggestions for further reading.

3. Starting with Isaac Newton's Law of Universal Gravitation (ca. 1667), many other theories have modified and expanded human understanding of the universe. Included among names frequently used are:

- Relativity (Albert Einstein, ca. 1916)
- Quantum mechanics (developed in 1920s)
- Uncertainty Principle (Werner Heisenberg, 1925)
- Chaos (Mitchell Feigenbaum, late 1970s, but with many other names also involved in this work)
- Grand Unified Theory (apparently a whole family of theories, recent date).

4   Darwinian Evolution

Writers outdo each other in finding words to express the technical excellence and intellectual importance of Charles Darwin's epochal works, *Origin of Species* (1859) and *The Descent of Man* (1871). There are a number of reasons for this. The voluminous data that Darwin gathered during five years as official naturalist aboard the H.M.S. *Beagle* (1831–36) represented a very high order of accomplishment in original research, both as to the quality of thought manifest in his work and as to the breadth and depth of coverage. The extent of his subsequent reading and the superb organization of his own and others' findings in support of his theory are apparently beyond words to praise. His well-reasoned and scientifically unassailable position was a haven of refuge and became a strong point for assault against the myrmidons of Protestant evangelical fundamentalism, which at the time held Britain and America in a sort of self-imposed intellectual slavery. Darwin's *Origin* served as an emancipation proclamation to those who chafed at this slavery.

Darwin was not alone, nor the first to do battle on behalf of "Hellenism" against "Hebraism."[1] While Darwin was still aboard the *Beagle*, Sir Charles Lyell (1797–1875) published his very popular and influential work, the *Principles of Geology*, in which he set forth scientifically defensible estimates as to the ages of various strata of rock going back to the Tertiary Period, about 70 million years ago. This was not nearly so dramatic as the astrophysicists' proof a century later that our universe is some 15–20 billion years old, but it did awaken thoughtful people to the idea that "everything the Bible says ain't necessarily so." Articulate fundamentalists within the Protestant evangelical ranks at that time deplored and denounced such publications as subversive nonsense, contrary to that obviously higher authority, the sacrosanct Word of God. However, scientists were to be held in contempt rather than feared.

Darwin's work followed by two and a half centuries the publication of Francis Bacon's *Novum Organum* (1620), arbitrarily taken as the beginning of the scientific era in the history of human thought. Sir Isaac Newton had worked out some of his great theories in 1664–66 and published his greatest work, *Mathematical Principles of Natural Philosophy*, in 1687.

It is probably more than random-chance type of coincidence that a great awakening of religious free thought had begun about the same time. George Fox founded the Society of Friends (Quakers) about 1650. The two Wesleys and the great hymn writer Isaac Watts polarized widespread religious fervor among the working and middle classes throughout Britain and North America all during the first half of the eighteenth century. Both the scientific and the religious movements represented a breaking with prevailing orthodoxy and a seeking new answers: the scientists through intellectual examination of phenomena observed in nature, and the religious nonconformists through personal emotional experience of the love of God through reading and preaching His holy word, the Bible.

By mid-nineteenth century, the religious movement had led to the emotional excesses of Protestant evangelical fundamentalism with its missionary outreach seeking to spread the light of "Christian civilization" to all parts of the world. "Faith" had reached tidal wave proportions. It was perhaps pure random chance that Darwin's work should have appeared at such a time. It would have been just as great a piece of work at any other time. A lesser work might have been engulfed by the tidal wave, or put aside to be rediscovered when the wave receded. As it was, the confrontation between revelation by scientific observation and revelation by Word of God became an issue that obsessed England and America for half a century: Hellenists versus Hebraism!

This bitter fight reached a sort of crisis or watershed in a small country courthouse in the State of Tennessee in 1925, 66 years after publication of *Origin of Species*. Tennessee is noted as a Bible-Belt state, and the voters in that state had succeeded in passing a law that prohibited the teaching in public schools of theories contrary to the Bible account regarding the creation of man. John T. Scopes, a biology teacher, deliberately violated that law and a trial ensued. Two famous public figures, Clarence Darrow for the defense and William Jennings Bryan for the state, gave their services to the respective sides, and the proceedings were followed nationally and internationally in the public press. Scopes was convicted as charged and sent to jail, but was soon released by the state's Supreme Court on the basis of a technical flaw in the proceedings. The law itself was not repealed until 1967. It may be said that the issue, which Darrow defined as free speech per se rather than the content of what was said, and which Bible-Belt citizens defined not as a question of fact but as respect for God, was never clearly settled. Other states that had similar legislation pending were influenced not to enact it. The general public, including loyal churchgoers, probably moved a step or two closer to Mr. Darwin.

The real issue (too bad it was not directly addressed) was the question as to relative authority and credibility of evidence gathered in the course of well-conducted, highly disciplined scientific research, when in conflict with a much rewritten (but very beautifully written) report of what a certain disembodied spirit is reputed to have said to certain spiritually gifted human beings well over 3,000 years earlier. A related but separate issue would have been: What constitutes respect for God and whose perception of God takes precedence in entitlement to respect?

As to these questions, there is not now and perhaps never will be a complete meeting of minds. Belief in the literal truth of everything one reads in the Bible is still shared by a surprisingly large number of people, who find security and comfort in that belief, namely, the fundamentalists of our time.

The issue attracts our attention today primarily in connection with its impact on our domestic and international politics—the political influence of the "moral majority" and "right to lifers," among the Christians, led by the Pat Robertsons, Jerry Falwells and others, and of course the fundamentalists' widespread support of Israel's claim to the land of Canaan "because God gave it to them; it says so in the Bible." Other religions have their fundamentalists too, ranging from quietists and mystics to activists and zealots: the Rabbi

Kehanes, the Menachem Begins, and the "hawks" of the Likud Party in Judaism, or the Ayatollah Khomeinis and the Muammar al-Qaddafis of Islam.

Darwin's theory of evolution is well known and needs no review or summary here. It presupposes the synthesis of life on Earth, an event that probably occurred between 4 and 6 billion years ago. Earth was then, say 10 billion years old and had cooled very much, although the climate and atmospheric conditions were not necessarily exactly as we know them now. Whatever the first life form may have been, and regardless of whether there was only one such event of synthesis or several, it or they had the property of renewing themselves by reproduction, and that process carried with it the possibility of genetic mutation. The following definition of mutation is provided by *The New Columbia Encyclopedia:*

. . . a sudden change in a gene, or unit of hereditary material, that results in a new inheritable characteristic. In higher animals and many higher plants a mutation may be transmitted to future generations only if it occurs in germ or sex cell tissue. . . .

The article explains that somatic or body-cell mutations can, however, be transmitted asexually by lower forms of life; this doubtless would apply to the earliest forms of life on Earth. The article goes on:

. . . A single gene mutation may have many effects if the enzyme it controls is involved in several metabolic processes. Many mutations are reversible, i.e., the mutant gene can revert to its previous form. Some genes are more unstable and susceptible to mutation than others so that repeated mutations of corresponding genes in different individuals may occur. . . . Mutations may be induced by exposure to ultraviolet rays and ionizing radiation from alpha, beta, gamma, and x-rays, by extreme changes in temperature, and by certain chemicals.

After discussing later studies and some of the technical aspects of mutation (i.e., later than Darwin's time), the article goes on again:

. . . Most mutations are lethal, since any changes in the delicate balance of an organism having a high level of adaptation to its environment tends to be disruptive. Of the few positive mutations, most are of recessive traits that are neutral in their effect on the organism and so can be retained without inhibiting its growth or reproductive processes. A change in the environment can encourage the survival of a dominant non-lethal mutation. Thus, hypothetically, a mutation caused in nature by the cumulative effect of ionizing radiation in the Earth's atmosphere might, with a coincidental change in the environment, give rise to a new species; this process is now believed to be a chief agent in the process of evolution and in the extinction of species that fail to mutate in a changing environment.[2]

And from the same source, under the article on *evolution:*

. . . the theory of evolution (as established by Darwin) . . . has undergone modifications in the light of later scientific developments. . . . The chief weakness of Darwinian evolution lay in its inability to explain satisfactorily the mechanism of evolution and of origin of species. Natural selection could explain why certain variations survived and others were lost, but not how these variations initially arose or were transmitted to offspring, and hence to subsequent generations. . . .

And touching on quasi-moral implications of the concept of evolution:

. . . A still prevalent misunderstanding of evolution is the belief that an animal or plant changes in order to better adapt to its environment. . . . Since mutation is a random process and since most mutations are harmful rather than neutral or beneficial to the organism, it is evident that the occurrence of a variation is itself a matter of chance, and cannot speak of a will or purpose on the part of the individual to develop a new structure or trait that might prove helpful . . . the notion that the struggle for existence means actual physical competition among individuals is erroneous. Evolution is a continuing process in which chance variations are constantly interacting with environmental conditions to determine the success of the individual and the species.

Our concern with Darwinian evolution consists, first, in the electrifying effect of Darwin's original proposal on human thinking in general, and second—as a reflective sort of afterthought—in what it tells us further about the essence and dynamism of the universe. The element of random chance, has played a major role as the universe unfolded itself following the big bang. It continues in evidence throughout the evolutionary development of plant and animal forms on the Earth. The more evidence one collects in this regard, the less viable becomes the concept that all these innumerable unpredictable happenings come from the mind of a disembodied, all-knowing, and all-powerful anthropomorphic spirit, a prototype human being, standing at some sort of drawing board and controls somewhere "up there," planning out every move for the ultimate well-being of people on Earth.

Enormous all-pervasive energy—always moving, always changing things—yes. But a nonmolecular, human-type brain standing at a cosmic drawing board thinking and planning, showing outrageous favoritism now one way, now the other, no!

NOTES

1. The terms Hellenism and Hebraism were popularized by the poet and critic Matthew Arnold (1822–88) as a way of identifying two divergent schools of thought among the general population of Britain and America, both flourishing vigorously in his time. On the one hand were people-oriented people and on the other were Bible-oriented people: humanists versus fundamentalists. It had little or nothing to do with race, and even cut across religious lines. The Hellenists would have looked to the Greek philosopher Protagoras (ca. 490–421 B.C.), or at least to his famous saying: "Man is the measure of all things," as their founder. They would have found in Jesus of Nazareth a kindred spirit because of his emphasis during his life upon what was in the individual's heart, versus the Pharisees' emphasis on superficial adherence to the *Law*, which primarily concerned itself with external morals and performance of ritual.

Ironically, Christ's ministry had by Arnold's time long since been institutionalized into a format that paralleled or out-distanced the Hebrew cult of Pharisees on their own grounds in this regard. Those whom Arnold characterized as Hebraists started with the Protestant evangelical reformers and would have included rigid followers of Roman Catholic doctrine, dogma, and ritual, by definition. It would have included, of course, the fundamentalists and orthodox among Jews, but other practicing Jews of more liberal bent would have been found among his Hellenists. The same with the more liberal and more people-oriented Protestants and Catholics.

2. This point is well illustrated by the consequences of some great natural disaster that struck the Earth about 60 million years ago: One theory posits a collision with one or more very sizable wandering asteroids, another a great blowoff of volcanic material. According to either theory, the Earth became enveloped in a dust cloud so thick that the sun's rays could not

penetrate. Climatic changes occurred. The lush tropical vegetation that had supported the dinosaurs for over 100 million years disappeared and with it the dinosaurs themselves. Destruction was not confined to dinosaurs. Estimates indicate that more than half of all life forms, primarily the larger, more complex forms, were destroyed at that time. Other explanations have been offered for the change of environment that brought about the disappearance of these life forms, but all agree that some such cataclysm occurred.

From our point of view, the importance of the event lies in the sweeping destruction caused by change of environment; it was not a competitive takeover by new, more effective competitors, but the destruction of organisms that, for perhaps 160 million years, had demonstrated highly efficient and effective adaptation to one environment but could not adapt to another. Survivors were the smaller, less highly specialized organisms and those whose recessive genes now served a useful purpose.

It is also illustrative of the incidence of random chance in the evolution of the universe. Had there been astrophysicists living in that mesozoic age, equipped with the knowledge and instrumentation available today, they might have been able to foresee an approaching collision, but not to avoid it. Had there been geophysicists equipped with greater knowledge than we have today regarding the movement of subsurface plates and other natural Earth forces, they might have been able to foresee a vast volcanic explosion (if that is what occurred), but could not have prevented it. It *is* possible that by foreseeing the event, they might have sheltered themselves, which is to say humankind, from extinction—and even perhaps have kept a few dinosaurs alive to continue the breed in special dinosaur preserves.

This event gives rise to speculation that has no part in our main discussion but may enliven (or even enlighten) our reading of the Noah myth. In that myth, the Lord became angry with all people on Earth because of their sins, and was determined to destroy them by flood. (The sin motif is prominent in Hebrew literature.) In Noah alone God found virtue and determined to save him along with certain animals to repopulate the world after the planned destruction. It was an excellent attention-getting story and carried a good moral lesson to all who heard it.

It may be interesting to play with an idea, which someone else may have suggested unknown to this writer, that this interplanetary collision (or whatever it was) and the ensuing carnage would have set the stage for the nearly worldwide distribution of legends of a catastrophic flood, of which the Noah story in our Bible is but one example.

When earliest human beings emerged on the scene almost 60 million years later, they would have observed unexplained deposits of bones, for example, on the plains of China and central Asia and elsewhere in the Old World, and in America, wherever climatic conditions did not lead to their earlier disintegration. Many would have been left by dinosaurs but also by other creatures, not all necessarily by creatures destroyed in that one catastrophic event.

Also, many areas now far from the ocean, often at considerable elevations, display fossils of ocean life, placed there by geologic upheavals eons earlier and having no necessary connection with the catastrophic event just mentioned. Primitive man could have attributed these evidences of widespread death to a flood that had covered the face of the Earth and then receded. The invention of flood legends to account for these phenomena would be a scientific error of course, but a not unreasonable attempt (*faute de mieux*) to establish a plausible explanation.

Some such factor may be more satisfactory to account for the wide dissemination of the flood myth, than the theory that it was carried by word of mouth when primitive man emigrated all over the world from a central location, for example, from Mount Ararat.

5   The Human Brain

To the inquiring historian, the brain is the source and fountainhead of all history, to the philosopher of all philosophy, to the aesthete of all beauty, to the mathematician of all mathematics, to the moralist of all value judgments, to the theologian of all religion, and so on. To the scientist the mind is the means of observation and the source of understanding about realities existing in the physical world (including of course the mind itself)—all are in final analysis to be regarded as manifestations of the omnipresent universal dynamism of the universe.

With its attendant facilities to communicate and (within reason) to accomplish what it sets out to do, the human brain is the first instrument or agency to emerge in the evolution of our Earth capable of observing, understanding, and utilizing (or in some cases deflecting) the effects of the creative, on-going, all-pervasive dynamism of which it is itself a manifestation. In this one respect human beings are, as we have noted, superior to their Creator, yet their Creator still holds the trump cards!

The full implications of this unique special ability are difficult to comprehend. Before human beings existed, the creative energy of the universe operated in a random, hit-or-miss manner. It still does, but human beings have the capability (at least with respect to materials and events that fall within their immediate reach) to reduce or eliminate the random chance element and replace it with planning and control.

Human beings too easily take this unique power over nature for granted without proper respect for the responsibility that goes with it, and especially without recognition of the unique power conferred through possession of a human brain. It is an option for people to decide whether to exercise this ability with far-sighted objectivity or short-sighted self-interest—insofar as one can foretell the consequences of interfering with the course of nature. The medical doctor, for instance, may interfere with the factor of random chance on behalf of his patient and arrange matters so as to maximize the beneficent positive elements in natural law and minimize the negative.

The human brain is the control for many of the human species' superior physical powers, for example, the power to walk upright, to talk, to manipulate fingers, and so on. It is the control for mental and emotional functions: thoughts, feelings, moods, moral and ethical judgments, and all that constitutes that very complex entity which we call soul or psyche. Some of these powers are shared with others among the higher animals; many are unique to human beings.

This statement has special implications for the "revealed" religions, Judaism, Christianity, and Islam, embracing as they do two-thirds of the world population. Messages formerly thought to have been sent from somewhere "up there" to special, highly gifted individuals allegedly chosen by God as His agents and accepted by people as prophets are now seen as originating deep within the subconscious psyche of those specially gifted individuals and then somehow, in the mysterious workings of the human mind, projected out and echoed back to a conscious level of that same psyche as the Word of God.

In seeking an illustrative parallel to this phenomenon, one thinks of the familiar navigational device, radar. A stream of electronic impulses is sent out, unperceived by human sense. Ions that encounter reflective materials come back almost instantaneously, and upon receipt, are electronically converted to a visible blip. The latter appears in a position on the radar screen, the movement of which enables the operator to determine direction and distance of the intercepted object from the transmitter. Thus transferred from imperceptible to perceptible, the information enters that ultimate computer, the human mind, where it is used to make correct decisions in steering ships, aircraft, etc. If the impulse had not been sent out, no reflection would have come back. Radar is itself a product of human genius, but it provides, beyond the capability of even the most gifted human mind to provide for itself, vision and guidance in fog or dark.

The theme of this chapter thus centers on the unique and, as yet, little comprehended physiology of the human brain, and the implications of that for a modern and forward-looking understanding of the role of human beings in the cosmic scheme of things. We begin with the words of Timothy A. Pedley, M.D., in his introduction to the section "Brain, Nerve, and Muscle Disorders" in the *Columbia University College of Physicians and Surgeons Complete Home Medical Guide*, a widely available reference source written for the layman:

Though modern medicine has an enormous array of measuring instruments, computers, and laser technology at its disposal and has made vast strides toward eliminating many of the maladies that afflict the human body, it has come up with nothing to match the overwhelming complexity of the human brain. This intimidating mass of grey matter, white matter, and electrical impulses, combined with the sprawl of the peripheral nerves interacting with the muscular system, creates an awe-inspiring synthesis of thought, emotion, and action with no apparent limits.

Dr. Pedley goes on to describe (with numerous diagrams) the various parts of the brain and in a general way the functions that each is believed to control.

Paul H. Wender and Donald F. Klein, professors of psychiatry, writing of "the revolutionary advances in biopsychiatry," in *Mind, Mood, and Medicine* (1982), have this to say regarding the physiology of the brain (p. 197):

. . . recent expansion of knowledge of brain physiology and chemistry . . . has been accumulating exponentially during the last twenty years. . . . Of special importance in the field of psychiatry are the conjectures concerning how nervous transmission may occur within the brain. The part of the brain that governs sensing, thinking, and feeling consists of at least 10 trillion cells. Each cell consists of a round body, microscopic in size, which contains much of the chemical machinery, and an extension, the axon (or wire) connecting the cell, in an incredibly complex manner, to hundreds or even thousands of other cells. The diameter of the axon is microscopic, but its length may be inches to feet. Coordinated brain activity is produced by the conduction or transmission of electrical impulses (discharge, or "firing") from one nerve cell to another by means of the axon. This process takes place, not only by simple electrical conduction, as with two copper wires that are touching each other, but, surprisingly, by chemical means.

Available evidence allows the following hypothesis about how chemical conduction from one cell to another may take place. When the first cell is stimulated, an electrical impulse travels the length of its axon and at the end discharges or releases a very small packet of chemicals known as neurotransmitters. When the neurotransmitters are released they drift rapidly across an extremely small space—the synaptic cleft—between the axon and the adjoining nerve cell, either stimulating that nerve cell, causing it in turn to fire, or inhibiting it, diminishing its ability to respond to stimulation by other nerve cells. . . .

In the last decade, researchers have also learned that there are a number of different neurotransmitters. . . . It is not clear whether each nerve cell releases only one sort of neurotransmitter or whether some cells release a mixture. . . .

This knowledge of chemistry helps us to understand the three major forms of genetically produced mental illness: (1) the disorders of mood, (2) several personality disorders . . . , and (3) the schizophrenias; in other words, how chemistry is related to sadness, badness, and madness.

Psychiatrists are interested in these matters from the point of view of restoring disordered brain functions to an acceptable level of normality. We are interested from the point of view of understanding the physiology of what one can only call the most marvelous, mysterious, comprehensive yet incomprehensible of all machines—the seat of all human volition and receiver certainly (and as we believe sender also) of those messages that in the prescientific era were attributed to divine revelation. Thus the human brain is seat of "God-in-here" regardless of what one may choose to believe regarding a "God-up-there."

It is interesting to note in passing that psychotherapy as developed by Freud and his followers relied on the ability of the human brain to correct its own chemical imbalances by conversational and/or emotional methods, apparently enlisting normal stimulants or inhibitors (presumed to be present somewhere) to prevail over the abnormal. That process is constantly taking place even (or especially) in normal healthy brains. Wender and Klein draw attention to the necessity for introducing drugs in treating patients who do not respond to regular psychotherapy. There are many different kinds of drugs, each effective in specific clinical situations, though perhaps harmful in other clinical situations and if used by people whose brains are "normal".

Here one comes across references to the role of electricity in the physiology of the brain, though no clear indication of the nature of its function is offered. Prewarned by discussion in the previous chapter of the importance of the electrical charges borne by sub-atomic particles, then in present context simplistically multiplying the number of particles in each atom, by the number of atoms in each molecule, by the number of molecules in each of 10 trillion neurons (brain cells), one comes up with a number of electrical impulses that is truly astronomic. This opens vistas of virtually unlimited combinations of impulses that might be employed in this drama—the physiological functioning of the brain.

This phenomenon (the function of electrical impulses in brain physiology) provides additional support for our hypothesis that energy is the essence of the universe and/or that matter is merely organized energy. Not only does this observation provide occasion to draw attention to the physiological link between the power that shapes the thoughts of people with that which moves the largest galaxies; it also draws attention to the fact that the human brain is the only organism now known to be constituted in such a way as to be able conceptually to recognize this quintessential power and in a practical way to use it (within limits of course) for human ends.

We read of new marvels of medical science, which has long been concerned with the physiology of the brain in connection with the treatment of a wide spectrum of disorders, but has been inhibited in its pursuit of experimental data by moral considerations. Experimenters obviously must differentiate treatment of human beings from that of laboratory animals (though various humane societies are seeking to remove that differentiation). Furthermore the brain is like no other organ in the body in that tissue taken from one part tells little or nothing about what is going on in some other part. Unlike liver tissue or lung tissue, for example, there is little or no homogeneity. However, new instruments provide new facilities yielding new insights, and effects produced by new varieties of drugs including radioactive tracers can be observed and documented. It is one of the most exciting new fields for scientific research.

All the higher animals have brains and some of them are quite complex, whether measured by physical examination in the laboratory or by observation of behavior in the field. Furthermore, specific patterns of behavior seem to be characteristic of specific species, suggesting a genetic factor in the composition and/or arrangements of neurons that control such matters. Well documented examples are abundant: the migratory patterns of different species of birds, and of whales, or turtles, or fish. Among admirers of field dogs, it is well known that some strains are natural pointers, others retrievers, others harriers and so on; they can be trained in various ways but their natural proclivities seem to be inherited, built in, or preprogrammed.

It is more difficult to make valid generalizations of this type about human beings, because their brains and their behavior patterns are more complex. Added to the spectrum of special physical capabilities (and limitations) genetically inherent in *Homo sapiens*, is the capacity to think in abstract conceptual terms. This of itself introduces another dimension with its own broad spectrum of possibilities. Certain mental patterns do seem to run in families: musical ability, literary ability, hand-eye coordination, and so forth. Exceptional ability and genius, however, seem more erratic in their appearance.

In the case of human beings, environmental factors often obscure—or, of course, may enhance—genetic factors in the development of the individual. One illustrative example would be the contrast between two individuals both with superior musical talent, one born and raised in a family which loved and lived music, the other in a family which was quite indifferent; one with encouragement and economic backing to study and practice music, the other without; one determined to succeed, the other indolent; and finally the job market: availability of attractive well-paying employment. If all these variables could be entered into a computerized input-output program, a bewildering array of possibilities for success or failure would appear.

The fact that people do have this capacity to think conceptually does not ensure that their thinking processes will necessarily be logical or valid, nor that the concepts they produce will be in accordance with scientifically verifiable reality. History has already established all of this. Some test of quality must be present, even though we do not have any satisfactory measures to apply. The fact is that there has been a pattern of cultural and intellectual advancement. One would like to report that the quality of human intellectual performance, even the quality of the mind itself, has improved step by step along with the enormous increase in volume of output and the progression of research efforts into more and more distant fields, up higher mountains. Among factors working in favor of progressively higher standards in scientific research would be availability of constantly improving instruments and laboratory facilities, more extensive basic research (the building blocks on which advanced research depends), new and more creative methodology, even popular interest in scientific development and support for scientific knowledge and understanding (most teams do better when they are being watched by a grandstand full of loyal fans).

Another factor (or non-factor) to which we must give at least passing attention is the possibility that personal ambition, peer competition and economic pressures or other forces may produce improvements in the actual physiological capacity of brains engaged in this research arena. Charles Darwin thought he had identified such a factor at work among a certain subspecies or race of finches in one of the smaller islands of the Galapagos group; they seemed to have developed different types of bills adapted to different food requirements—a genetic adaptation not involving anything so fundamental as mutation. This finding has attracted considerable discussion in scientific circles and we leave it there. Turning to the world of sports and to the book of world records, evidence indicates that human beings do somehow manage to keep breaking records generation after generation. Some of this may be traced to better equipment, some to better training. We would like to attribute some of it to genetically improved physical capabilities induced by concentration on certain specific tasks, and then propose possible parallels between improving muscle tissue and the much more complex functions going on in human brains as a result of scientific research.

These matters are, however, peripheral to our central theme that the human brain is the seat of all human religious proclivities, and that these proclivities in turn are vitally and inextricably interrelated with the complex motivations and responses that shape history. Social, political, economic, cultural, and all other aspects of human activity, directly or indirectly, in some ways influence and in other ways are influenced by the innate religiosity of the human animal. From earliest times, long before written history, human beings have been creatively activated by this innate religiosity. They have endowed sticks, stones, places, meteorological phenomenon, idols, icons, and every imaginable formulation of unseen beings with supernatural properties that somehow relate back to themselves. This has been going on for many thousands of years, with the evidence going back at least as far as the cave paintings of southern France, and in archaeological discoveries perhaps earlier.

Within very recent times, scientific observations and the conclusions drawn from them have made it evident that those projections of supernatural properties into external objects or unseen beings are precisely that—projections—and that the real source of these perceptions of outer gods lies within the people themselves, specifically within the mysterious and incredibly complex formulations of the human brain.

The very suggestions of such an idea is threatening, but it should not be. Scientific realities have not changed in any way. It is the informed public's perception of reality which has changed, and much for the better! It calls for rereading the Bible and the Quran now not as immutable truth sent down from somewhere "up there" but as works of very great human geniuses by and about people whose lives provide guidance and inspiration. However, they are essentially human documents, not divine in the supranatural connotation of that word.

Of course, the word divine has other connotations. It would be perfectly correct and acceptable to say of the Bible and Quran (certain parts of them at least)—as one would say of a Beethoven symphony well-performed, or of a Rembrandt painting, or of an architectural masterpiece: a Parthenon, Taj Mahal, or Chartres Cathedral, or of a beautiful sunset, or even of one's newborn child— that it is divine! Each acquires its right to that designation primarily from its effect on the beholder. To be sure the genius of the artist is also recognized as in itself divine. Either way, "divinity" in this context is, as previously emphasized, a product of innate sensitivity and environmental preconditioning in the human mind.

We read in the Bible of the dreams and other communications conferred by the Lord on Abraham. Earlier appearances of the Lord as a familiar figure who walked and talked with Adam and others must be considered purely mythological. Patriarchs such as Abraham (ca. 1,800 B.C.) and Moses (ca. 1,250–1,200 B.C.) must be regraded as semilegendary. The Lord allegedly spoke to Moses somewhere between 1,500 and 2,000 times as reported in the first five books of the Bible, the subject matter of His communication ranging from the extremely important (e.g., the Ten Commandments) to the picayune or purely self-serving. Biblical scholarship identifies the pens of a half-dozen or so different writers in this material, ranging from one who wrote during the tenth century B.C. to one who seems to have been writing during the Babylonian Captivity (586–538 B.C.). Inquiring historians feel professionally obligated to ask themselves whether this is good history, and to communicate to their readers their evaluation as to the probability that the Lord in reality spoke the words attributed to Him, or that they were put in His mouth by later scribes.

One thing may be said with certainty: the all-important physiological function of a human brain was involved in any such revelation, religious experience,[1] vision, dream, or whatever. This would be true whether the religious experience actually occurred to Moses in his lifetime or to a gifted scribe 600 years later with retroattribution to Moses. Whatever the source of the stimuli received, the physiological sequence of events in the recipient's brain involved rapidly progressing rearrangements of neurons in response to some sort of stimulus or stimuli.

The innumerable stories one hears about supranatural happenings, include the many varieties of religious experience, but are not limited to that. Each must be screened for clues as to the circumstances in which the event happened and the credibility of the narrator. Some will be discarded. Others must be recognized as very real *for the person involved*, even if of doubtful authenticity for others. One person's brain actually produced the impressions reported as the Word of God or whatever, even though other brains possibly in the same room at the same time experienced no similar reaction. The most forceful statement of this phenomenon has already been quoted in a different context:

Jesus answered them, "Have faith in God. I tell you this: if anyone says to this mountain, 'Be lifted from your place and hurled into the sea,' and has no inward doubts, but believes that what he says is happening, it *will be done for him.* I tell you, then, whatever you ask for in prayer, *believe that you have received it and it will be yours . . ."*

(Mark 11:23–24; New English translation; author's italics).

This was cited earlier as an example, the ultimate example perhaps, of personal faith as belief in the untrue. But it is also an affirmation that supranatural events can be very real for the person who experiences them. It carries the strong further implication that human beings would have some optional control over the rapidly progressing rearrangements of neurons that take place within their brains in response to whatever stimulus or stimuli the receptors and neurotransmitters bring to it.

Where the mistaken perceptions of reality are voluntary—and/or classified as religious experience in the sense that William James used that term—they are within most people's definition of sanity. If not, call the psychiatrist!

Widespread interest in various forms of transcendental escape from worldly burdens and responsibilities (as some skeptics would put it), or direct experience of God (as religious mystics of Judaism, Christianity, and Islam would put it), or realization of the inner self through contemplation and meditation (as practitioners of Yoga, or followers of Ramakrishna and Zen might put it) bespeaks the reality and importance of man's ability to control the activity of certain neurons in his brain without use of drugs.[2] The catalog of physical and mental exercises employed to produce such results is long: deep breathing, chanting mantras, swaying in unison, twirling, to mention a few.[3] Long discussions may be held as to the therapeutic value of such experiences upon the practitioners' general mental health, which bespeaks linkages to other "teams" of neurons not directly involved in the transcendental experience.

It remains to speak of one more possible property or power of the human brain, perhaps shared by the brains of other animals, and that is the power to communicate with others' brains by extrasensory means. Examples of such communication may be seen in destructive mob action at one end of the scale, and in the dynamic serenity of a "gathered" meeting among members of the Society of Friends (Quakers) at the other end. The action of large flocks of birds or schools of fish turning and wheeling as though they had a single mind may be another. Stories of close relatives, mothers and sons, twin brothers, or the like, sensing that something terrible had happened just at the time when something terrible did in fact happen to the other, even halfway around the globe, are too persistent to be totally disregarded.

The neurosciences are scarcely beginning to unfold new understandings about the physiology of the brain. Where this understanding will lead is uncertain. One can reiterate with considerable certainty, however, that all of human thought, feeling, planning, communication, image-making, and all such matters, are products of the physiology of the human brain, acted upon by any imaginable stimulus, internal or external. Without specialized molecules formed into neurons and their related neurotransmitters, performing their proper functions within the brain there can be no thought, no feeling, no emotion, no image, no intelligible communication, etc. Long before these theories were evolved, the poet Thomas Gray (1716–1771) unwittingly asserted this scientific fact, namely that an "experience" cannot happen without the interposition of a human brain to receive and process the stimuli. He enriched the statement of this scientific truth with a brilliant brocade of imagery and beauty of expression which no scientist would hope to achieve:

> Full many a gem of purest ray serene
> The dark unfathomed caves of ocean bear:
> Full many a flower is born to blush unseen
> And waste its sweetness on the desert air.
>
> *Elegy Written in a Country Churchyard*

This chapter may close as it opened, with the observation that the human mind is a truly miraculous instrument, unique on Earth. It is the seat equally of our species' purely animal instincts; of our mundane decision-making functions; of highest achievements in abstract thought; of mystic religious experiences; and of feelings of humanity, compassion, fair play, honesty, and other distinctively human virtues (a group of qualities that somehow come together under the catchwords "psyche" or "soul"). Enconiums about the potentialities of the mind must be tempered by recognition of its bestial potentialities also, but an individual has considerable control over what the mix will be, as between animal and spiritual elements.

To summarize, the mind is a divine gift, the gift of the universal dynamism that we shall discuss in the next chapter. It is the ultimate determinant of human religious (as well as other) experiences, the monitor of our value systems. People must look "in here" rather than "up there" for ultimate authority in what they want to do, or for justification in what they have done. The "in-here" concept gives rise to Chapters 7 and 8.

NOTES

1. William James (1841–1910), *The Varieties of Religious Experience*. First published in 1902, this work has been republished many times, with various editors and commentators. James's observations have many applications throughout the present paper.

One cannot avoid speculating whether, if James were writing today, he would carry his subject one long step further by discussing the physiology of religious experience in terms of the exciting new observations and experiments mentioned above.

His book is based on a series of lectures given before a presumably highly intelligent and influential audience at the University of Edinburgh, at a time when the pendulum of intellectual and spiritual thought—the *zeitgeist* of the industrializing nations of Europe and America—was swinging away from what one may call Protestant pharisaism (belief in the literal truth of every word in the Bible, compulsive church attendance, fervent missionary zeal, and all that followed from that) toward an attitude of uncertainty, a growing realization that Darwin was right. For some, one faith had been shattered and another was not yet at hand. James's objective seems to have been to slow the swing of this pendulum by asserting that religious experience *is* a scientifically recognizable psychological phenomenon, a very real and potent factor in the lives of many people, not to be dismissed as "queer."

We shall never know to what extent the immediate popularity of his lectures was due to his skill and charisma as lecturer, and/or to the relief of distressed minds to find a haven of security in James's assurances that religious experience was valid at a time when the old security of implicit belief in infallibility of biblical revelation had been, for them, blown away by Darwin's theories and the ramifications thereof.

For purposes of this book, we would like to add the thought that earliest human beings, long before religious systems involving "revelation" and other complex theological apparatus had been developed, undoubtedly experienced a variety of strange emotional stimulations: dreams and ecstatic experiences especially, some perhaps sex-related, plus occasional psychiatric derangement, unexplainable twitches and other sensations, all perceived as visitations by spirits. James and his followers would probably classify at least some of these as religious experiences. Such "experiences" are not necessarily limited to *Homo sapiens*. Similar stimuli can be inferred from behavior of dogs, cats, horses, and so forth. However, the ability to formulate such experiences into visions of good and evil spirits, and ultimately into the concept of an anthropomorphic God, is uniquely human.

2. The variety of stimuli to which human beings can be exposed or can deliberately arrange for the purpose of producing one or another variety of religious experience should be the subject of a separate dissertation. One of the oldest known examples of this activity and one of the most moving would be the Eleusinian Mysteries, taken over by the Athenians about 600 B.C. from certain families in Eleusis, who had probably performed some sort of agricultural rites in that location for many centuries before that. The ritual celebrated the abduction and return of Persephone.

Under Athenian sponsorship the rites were held every year, but no one who had participated once was ever permitted to repeat the experience. Those to be initiated were given an extensive preparation, whose details were shrouded in a secrecy perhaps comparable to Masonic and similar rites in our times. After a period of initiation into every aspect of the mysteries, lasting apparently several months and held at quarters in Athens, the initiates, perhaps in the thousands, walked the five to seven miles to Eleusis. There they participated in the preparation of a special drink containing, it is thought, a hallucinogenic drug based on ergot of barley. After drinking of this brew and participating in special rites until it had taken effect, they were introduced into the sacred chamber.

What ceremonies and stage effects were employed there is at best a matter of speculation, but by many reports it was a very, very impressive experience, from which men and women returned, as it were, spiritually drained and refilled.

It was part of the mystique for the initiates to maintain silence regarding the details of their experience. This especially challenges the curiosity of modern man. Several books have been written on the subject. Among the most recent is *The Road to Eleusis/Unveiling the Secret of the Mysteries*, by R. Gordon Wasson, Carl A. P. Ruck, and Albert Hofmann (1978). Wasson was the discoverer of ancient hallucinogenic mushroom cults in Mexico, from which the synthetic LSD was developed. Hofmann is the Swiss chemist who in 1942 synthesized LSD. Ruck is a professor at Boston University specializing in Greek ethnobotany (ancient Greek wines, for example, always contained other stimulants besides alcohol). His special contribution to this work carries abundant footnotes referring to many scholarly sources.

3. Among the most familiar and effective neuron-organizing effects, very

extensively utilized for religious purposes, but not only for that, is the playing of beautiful music, or the resonance of the well-modulated human voice reading familiar works (even when the hearer is inclined to discount the merit of what is being said). John Milton expresses this as follows:

> But let my due feet never fail
> To walk the studious cloister's pale
> And love the high-embowéd roof,
> with antique pillars massy proof
> And storied windows richly dight
> casting a dim religious light:
> There let the pealing organ blow
> To the full-voiced choir below
> In service high and anthems clear,
> As may with sweetness, through mine ear,
> Dissolve me into ecstacies,
> And bring all Heaven before mine eyes.
>
> *Il Penseroso*

One may say with tongue in cheek: how beautiful and awe-inspiring is the work of the neurons as they affect the activity of other neurons, in special ways in response to this sort of stimuli received via the central nervous system, work done with the speed of light traveling over very short distances!

Milton's poem calls attention to some of the sorts of stimuli that could and did produce a transcendental effect through activity of neurons within one very sensitive and very gifted brain. Today, the reading of it evokes pleasurable reactions within the brains of each individual reader, depending on the preprogramming of each brain and the richness of the memories stored up and accessible (not all memories are readily accessible) within it. Each individual thereby enjoys the beauty of the words themselves and the images that the words conjure up in a uniquely personal way.

One also thinks of other, historically more important, effects achieved by an eloquent speaker or writer. For example, Anthony's funeral oration, playing on the emotions of the Roman rabble at Caesar's burial, which brought Augustus Caesar to power and established imperium at Rome; Urban II's speech to the Council of Claremont in 1095, which touched off the great Crusading movement; the enormously popular book, *Uncle Tom's Cabin*, by Harriet Beecher Stowe, which polarized northern sentiment at the time of the U.S. Civil War, and many others. Despite whatever value judgments one may pass upon these examples, the scientific fact is that they all depended for their effect on their ability to evoke particular neuronal activities within human brains.

One may hazard a tentative generalization that no religious movement ever reached greatness, or long survived, without an eloquent and charismatic prophet who wrote or inspired a "divine" book of highest literary quality. In this, one places emphasis on the pure musical and poetic quality of cadences in the words spoken or written, rather than on the intellectual quality of the message that they convey, although the latter is of course important. Many a meritorious message may be lost through lack of adequate vehicle to convey it. Probably the converse is also true; many banal or mischief-working thoughts are enshrined by the power and beauty of the words in which they are conveyed.

The first and some would say greatest literary works in the Greek language are the *Iliad* and *Odyssey*, which, arguably, may be taken as the "Bible" of the Greco-Roman religion. Our Bible serves that function for the Judeo-Christian religions. Without passing judgment on the variable merits of the thoughts expressed, one must recognize that just hearing or reading the familiar and beautiful words—in the original for those who understand them, or in one of the familiar and well-loved translations—is in itself a sort of activator that induces an aesthetic/religious experience in the mind of the hearer or reader.

Even more so the Quran, which, like the *Iliad* and *Odyssey*, not only introduced a new religion but also a new language. Whether or not one accepts the religious message as sacred truth, the person who hears what is alleged to be the Word of God spoken so beautifully cannot but be moved. The medium itself may be characterized as "divine."

6   Man's Options and How
       He Got Them

The emergence of human beings with their unique mental powers marks an entirely new era in the cosmic scheme of things. Never before on Earth had there been creatures with anything like the options now open to humans. One can say with almost equal certainty that there never has been such a creature anywhere within our solar system. What may exist elsewhere is in the province of science fiction.

The most dramatic of the options, of course, is human beings' newly acquired destructive power, utilizing nuclear weaponry. We probably do not yet have the power to destroy all human life simultaneously—and all other life in the process—but that will come. One may say hopefully and prayerfully that such an option would never be exercised, but the possibilities are scary—one suicidal maniac, brooding on the miseries of a world population (by that time of say 10 or 15 billion), all struggling to control a larger and larger portion of shrinking food supplies and dwindling natural resources, a maniac who would come to the conclusion that the best way out is to end it all . . . and who would have access to the means whereby that could be done!

The offsetting options are, of course, a sensible use of nuclear energy as a necessary supplement to dwindling fossil fuels and to curb atmospheric pollution. We must utilize advancing technology: (1) to make nuclear power generation even safer than it already is in well-designed, well-built, and well-managed nuclear generating plants; and (2) to dispose of the radioactive waste wisely. Human beings already have exceptional technological capabilities in this regard, for example, to send such material to the sun (itself a sort of nuclear generating plant, which has been dealing with such materials for billions of years), and other possibilities, each to be weighed as to safety and economic feasibility.

However, these newest and most dramatic of human beings' unique options are cited only to focus attention on the extent and seriousness of our decision-making responsibility. We shall be especially interested in any genetic equipment we may have within ourselves and any help we can secure from outside to make the right decisions.

Meanwhile, we must have clearly in mind the newness of this new innovation (that is to say, *Homo sapiens*) in the cosmic scheme of things. Taking the figure of 15 billion years as the approximate age of the universe from the big bang to the present (this figure is widely accepted, but one finds occasional references to 20 billion years, and Hawking mentions 10 billion), one undertakes to translate that into some measure that the human mind can more easily comprehend. Readily at hand is the six-day period within which, according to the biblical myths, the Lord created the world. On a six-day scale, each day is equivalent to 2.5 billion years, each hour to somewhat more than 100 million years, each minute to almost 2 million years, and each second to almost 30,000 years.

Modern man, exemplified by the creators of the cave paintings in France, Spain, and in Africa, emerged only 35,000 years ago. That is one second out of six days and it is necessary to shift to milliseconds (thousandths of a second) in tracing human progress thereafter.

Starting with the big bang at 0001 Monday morning, all of that day, Tuesday, Wednesday, and Thursday were occupied by the cooling off and sorting out process; formation of comets, solar systems, galaxies, all constantly moving farther away from each other in general but pursuing individual courses that resulted in innumerable collisions. The layman sees this process as a sort of "battle royal" in which a number of fighters enter a ring, and at a signal, start knocking each other down. The last man standing wins the prize. Astrophysicists could explain it in much more dignified terms, of course, and would emphasize that the game had rules that were obeyed. However, they would agree that random chance played a very large part. Cosmic evolution was largely a hit-and-miss procedure; that is, there would be no predictability which astral body would hit which other one, nor what the consequences would be.

Sometime on the fifth day, which is to say sometime between early morning and noon on Friday, the Earth had become cool enough and all the other conditions were right (necessary materials were at hand and presumably collected together in one place) so that synthesis of life could occur, and it did occur. One may speculate whether conditions had been right prior to that moment while the critical spark (or whatever it was—some agency from outside) had not happened, or whether it occurred by a sort of spontaneous combustion from the materials themselves. What form that initial living organism took is still a matter of speculation—possibly some form of lichen or a protozoan of some kind.

The remaining 12–18 hours on Friday and at least 23 of the available 24 hours on Saturday were taken up with the gradual development of the diverse plant and animal forms that came to cover the Earth. Development was by a process of evolution involving the phenomenon to which we have already made reference: mutations in cells responsible for reproduction, followed by a "testing" against the harsh realities of prevailing ecological environments. Mutations occurred with great frequency; successful mutations, very rarely (relatively speaking). It was largely a hit-and-miss procedure; there was little predictability as to where, when, or what kind of mutation would occur, but the rules of the game were fairly well set as to whether it would survive. Odds were very strongly against survival.

Later, we shall hope to develop the point that humans alone among all creatures ever to appear on Earth have power to change those odds, and are even taking tentative steps to control mutations.

Paleontology, the science of determining early life forms by means of fossil remains and all other sources of evidence, has made great progress in reconstructing the development of new life forms adapted to environmental conditions prevailing from time to time. That research is a two-way street; the fossil remains tell us something about what the environment must have been as well as vice versa. Somewhere in northern Australia a living organism has been found that closely matches fossil remains known to be 3 billion years old.

At about 2320 on Saturday evening, which is to say, with only 40 minutes remaining in the six-day week, a major catastrophe occurred (to which we have already made reference), which wiped out two-thirds of the Earth's animal population.

It is known that one variety of primates had evolved prior to this disaster, which is to say about 70 million years ago. These were small insectivores, rather like modern tree shrews, and they survived the holocaust. No direct genetic succession between that form of primate or later hominid primates and modern man has been established, but it is in this direction to which humans must look for their remote predecessors.

The earliest hominids would have appeared about two minutes ago on the six-day scale; *Homo erectus* one minute ago; the earliest examples of *Homo sapiens* as much as ten seconds ago; and Cro-Magnon man, whom many laymen regard as earliest prototype of modern "thinking man," one second ago. We simply do not know about human migrations that long ago. It seems unreasonable to postulate that Cro-Magnon man was the ancestor of *all* modern thinking men everywhere on Earth. Hence we shall presume parallel genetic development of the species, for example, in India, China, and Mesoamerica. Whatever his ancestry, thinking man is a very recent arrival upon the cosmic stage.

All earlier hominids, such as *Homo erectus* and Neanderthal man, have long since died out or lost identity through intermarriage. Thus, only *Homo sapiens* remains. This classification must be said to embrace all humankind, including very advanced and civilized groups with their intellectual achievements and quotas of outstanding genius, to other developing groups who have as yet shown little evidence of abstract thought.

New, significantly higher levels of culture appeared almost simultaneously in centers as far separated as China, India, Mesopotamia, Egypt, and Mesoamerica, perhaps 10,000 to 12,000 years ago. Whether there was any interregional communication to help account for the coincidence of significant cultural advances in such far-separated places at that time is debatable. Later, of course, armies and trade caravans did carry cultural elements over long distances. Alternatively, one may speculate that some waves of cosmic dynamism beyond the realm of human beings' present observation or comprehension would account for periods of global intellectual and cultural advance. If that hypothesis is accepted, one must also look to the same "cosmic dynamism" for other periods of stagnation.

Twelve thousand years would equate with 360 milliseconds, slightly over a third of a second on our six-day scale. Moses and Muhammad, the two great "revealers" of God-given law, lived 100 and 48 milliseconds ago, respectively. Aristotle, whose writings provided the basis for so many of the scientific and quasi-scientific studies, treatises, and speculations down to recent times, lived about 76 milliseconds ago. The threshold of the new modern scientific age is marked by publication of Francis Bacon's *Novum Organum* (1620), 12 milliseconds ago. Darwin's crucial work appeared four milliseconds ago, and the big bang theory, less than two.

By any scale, whether one speaks in terms of 35,000 years out of 15 billion, or one second out of six days, modern man is a very recent arrival—a statement that evokes a latent concern as to how long he will last. The answer doubtless depends largely on himself.

Even that short term of occupancy in this unique planet seems long in relation to the period of truly modern man's mastery through scientific knowledge over many of the functions and happenings impelled by the creative and on-going energy of which we have so often spoken. The dawn of the scientific era, arbitrarily set at A.D. 1620, occurred 268 years ago (12 milliseconds on the six-day scale). The almost explosive expansion of scientific knowledge over the past century, and especially over the past few decades, can hardly be measured by the flick of an eyelash on the six-day scale.

These perspectives on cosmic time are not exactly new or original. One may recall the familiar verses written 250 years ago by the prolific hymn writer Isaac Watts (1674–1748), from his hymn, "Oh God, our help in ages past:"

> Before the hills in order stood
> Or earth received her frame
> From everlasting Thou art God,
> To endless years the same.

> A thousand ages in Thy sight
> Are like an evening gone;
> Short as the watch that ends the night
> Before the rising sun.

To be sure, the Reverend Watts did not pinpoint the date when the Earth (he uses a small letter "e") received her frame, nor differentiate (as we feel necessary to do) between the eternal and all-pervasive, mindless force manifest in all creation and evolution, vis-à-vis the man-centered perceptions and resultant images of an anthropomorphic supreme being or beings formulated in the minds of humans after their emergence into the cosmic scene.

To anticipate a thesis dealt with more fully below, the issue is not at all a question of different entities but of one entity differently perceived. In this respect, humans find themselves in almost exactly the same situation as that which gave rise to the well-known parable of the nine blind men who had examined an elephant and came away with total disagreement as to the nature of the beast.

Many writers have developed this theme to emphasize how insignificant humans really are in the cosmic scheme of things: an accidental product of an impartial and inexorable evolutionary process, stuck on one small planet among many billions of similar bodies, in one remote corner of the universe, and with nowhere to go:

> Oh, why should the spirit of mortal be proud?
> Like a swift-flitting meteor, a fast-flying cloud,
> A flash of the lightning, a break of the wave,
> He passeth from life to his rest in the grave.
> > (By William Knox. This was the favorite hymn of
> > Abraham Lincoln.)

It is to be hoped that the above recital of the scientists' evolution story will now produce the opposite reaction: how remarkable that we are here! How exciting! What marvelous possibilities, if we just don't goof!

7   The All-Pervasive Force, Essence
of the Universe—Deus
Universalis

Objective scientific observations of the type reviewed herein do not invalidate but, on the contrary, confirm people's age-old awareness of a supreme being. However, they must change human perceptions as to the nature of that being and of people's own relationship to it. They bring out a scenario in which—following the generally accepted big bang theory—the universe was formed some 15 or 20 billion years ago and has gone on developing ever since, impelled by a power so vast and all-pervasive that it is beyond human comprehension or explanation. Nor do human beings need to comprehend or explain. It just is—always has been, and always will be.

Though human beings cannot comprehend or explain, they can establish certain peripheral theories regarding the nature and functions of this power. Such theories may be characterized as declarations of faith (in the "working hypotheses" sense of that word). They are statements regarding the unknown, perhaps unknowable; they may be stepping stones toward a better understanding, but never assertions of sacrosanct verity. They represent a replacement or radical updating of scenarios once formulated to answer questions generated by people's earliest observations and experiences, scenarios that are now seen to be erroneous in light of recent scientific probings into the origin and nature of the universe.

The universal, all-pervasive force of which we speak is, as herein repeatedly stated, manifest in all matter in every form, from the stars in the sky and oldest granite of the hills to the most ephemeral living tissue—from objects that are large and visible to sub-microscopic organisms and viruses—in other words, in all substances living and dead, all being comprised of molecules and they, in turn, comprised of atoms and they, in turn, of tiny particles bearing electric charges held together in infinitely varied groupings. The same force is manifest also in all intangible physical forces, for example, electricity, light, sound, gravity, inertia, radioactivity, centrifugal force, all the branches of thermodynamics, and so on. It is a force that governs the movements of stars and the dynamics of individual atoms, a force that presumably existed before the big bang and would continue to exist even though the universe were to disappear in a reverse big crunch.

This universal force is marked, as previously noted, by the consistency with which matter (molecular substances) and nonmolecular energy behave when subjected to certain environmental conditions, but equally characterized by the happenings that can only be attributed to random chance. It is the latter that seems to have brought various substances together at particular times and places, and thus determined the nature and potential of different astral bodies. Random chance is seen in the occurrence of the mutations by which life on Earth has become so varied, and therefore in the eventual emergence of human beings and their remarkable brains.

This all-pervasive force has no anthropomorphic characteristics whatsoever. For one thing, the facts of cosmic evolution are quite at variance with modern man's natural and normal concepts of wise planning and good executive management by a kindly and forgiving, all-knowing and all-powerful anthropomorphic divine being, one who has human beings constantly in mind among His many responsibilities. It would be the height of irreverence to attribute to such an idealized God the harshness and cruelty and waste of evolution, wherein a profusion of nonviable organisms are created only to be destroyed, or the haphazard and sometimes catastrophic effects of collisions among astral bodies. If the Creator had a brain and a psyche like the Earth-creature who claims to have been made in His image, He would at least have *tried* to be more efficient and get things right in the first place! Being all-knowing and all-powerful, He should have succeeded in that effort!

Even Muhammad, who vigorously asserted the principle that Allah could not be compared to any living person or to anything whatsoever, nevertheless delineated a being whose language was exclusively Arabic, whose 99 alternate names included virtually the entire gamut of preferred human characteristics, and whose messages to the people bespoke a relatively humane and worldly wise legislator full of wise admonitions appropriate to a pastoral-nomadic and mercantile people such as those among whom it was promulgated.

In the present state of scientific knowledge, one can only characterize the universal force of which we are speaking as pure energy, dynamism, vitality—undirected, impersonal, impartial, unthinking, uncaring, neither merciful nor cruel, unaware of (and certainly taking no pleasure nor feeling any remorse over) the effects of its own power, unchangeable, yet constantly causing changes to occur, present in all matter and in all intangible forces of nature, inexorable, eternal. It is a force that acts in predictable ways yet produces results about which there is no predicting.

If comparison can be made one would select one of the component manifestations of this universal force, electricity—the force that powers whatever machine or heats up whatever resistant material it encounters, but has no independent plan and does not exercise any discretion nor pass any judgments upon the merit of the machines it powers or the work they do. It is a force that human beings can harness for innumerable useful purposes, yet which can equally prove harmful.

For convenience of reference, we shall designate this vast, eternal dynamism, which is the essence of all and upon which all depends, as Deus Universalis.

8 Thinking Man Requires a Thinking God—Deus Sapiens

Humankind is a religious animal—some more and some less religious. No matter where the individual fits along the familiar bell-shaped curve (which we presume, could be constructed as a hypothetical gauge of sensitivity to religious matters), there are times when each man and each woman wants to and needs to relate to some abstract higher being, in joy or sorrow, in praise or penitence, as one who has desperate needs or wants desperately to share. Every religious system devised by people, from the most primitive totemism to the most esoteric mysticism or the cleverest of Byzantine theological sophistry, is the result of human beings' innate desire and need to relate to such a being.

How can one have a personal relationship to an impersonal force such as that delineated in the previous chapter? Deus Universalis, is to be sure, the vital force upon which human beings depend for life itself and for the ability to perform every act, to think every thought, and to feel every feeling. Every organism, all inert matter, and all the various forces of nature have the same relationship, and are equally "important" or "unimportant" to such a being.

Human beings can uniquely relate to such a power by learning to understand and utilize materials that it has formed and the natural forces that it has set in motion: electricity, and energy in other forms such as heat, light, radioactivity, gravity, and so on through a long list. However, these intellectual "relationships" do not satisfy human beings' religious nature and need for a personal relationship.

This is a uniquely human problem. Until our species emerged onto the cosmic stage, there was no such need, no awareness of a creator, and no religious nature needing gratification in this way. Historically, creation of the problem sets in motion the process of its solution. The process is still going on. The solutions arrived at up to the present time have been as diverse as humankind is diverse. Some solutions, though meritorious in themselves, have produced unfortunate and indeed deadly side effects. This work offers no positive new solutions, but draws attention to dangers inherent in some, at least of the solutions that human beings have worked out in the past. It focuses attention hopefully on the vastly superior resources of modern scientific observation and historical scholarship, vis-à-vis blind faith in outmoded myths, as a channel whereby to establish more efficacious solutions with fewer harmful side effects.

Human beings' unique intellectual capacity and psychological constitution is a product of the dynamism of the force that we have designated as Deus Universalis. It contains elements arguably superior to, yet still totally dependent on, that force. Given this remarkable intellectual-cum-religious facility, humans have been able to sense the presence of some eternal universal force greater than themselves, but only in terms of their own experience and nature. Human beings (some of them at any rate) have created images of a God very like themselves, only better and stronger. They had no other pattern to follow.

The diversity and changeability of people's deity concepts detract from their credibility. Their deities tell different people different things at different times. Obviously they are not "immutable," nor "eternal" in that respect—and they can't all be right! Yet the verifiable fact—one may call it a common denominator—that virtually all humankind has sensed the existence of some sort of spiritual superpower strengthens the impartial observer's conviction that some such entity does exist, and must be accounted for as a scientific reality, however imperfectly perceived by human beings.

Concepts of God began with the advent of thinking man, *Homo sapiens*, rather than the other way around. If people were to disappear from the cosmic scene, their perceptions and images would disappear with them, including, of course, their concept of a thinking, man-oriented, anthropomorphic God. That event would leave the universe where it was before human beings arrived, to continue its eternal, inexorable progress in its own characteristic hit-or-miss fashion, impelled by the universal, all-pervasive dynamism of which we have spoken so often, Deus Universalis. Thus, we must introduce a recognition of "double vision" in people's awareness of a Supreme Being. There is, first, the all-pervasive, eternal energy or dynamism of the universe, devoid of human characteristics, the Deus Universalis; and there is, second, a complex man-made spiritual dimension existing by reason of "thinking man's" existence and just as "real" as humans themselves are real—Deus Sapiens, God of many aspects, as diverse yet unitary as *Homo sapiens*.

The man-made, man-centered, God images usually represent a sort of apotheosis of people's upward yearnings and aspirations, their source of solace in bereavement, of forgiveness from sin, and so forth. These images are endowed with virtues and ideals in accordance with the various human value systems. To have value systems is characteristic of human existence, but the systems themselves are as ephemeral as human thinking (though usually deemed to be eternal).

The merit of that "eternal" presumption must be examined. It depends on the time horizon that people attach to the word "eternity." Value systems can change several times within an individual's lifetime, or may last for several generations. The religious propensity that we take to be one of the genetic characteristics distinguishing our species from other animals, has lasted, so far, perhaps 35,000 years or perhaps 2,000,000, depending on the starting point. We hope it will last many millions more, but it is not inherently "eternal." Only Deus Universalis is truly eternal.

To the extent that human beings insist on an exclusively idealistic image for their God, it is necessary to associate with God an evil partner: the Devil, Satan, Iblis, or whatever. This seems somewhat inconsistent with the general monotheistic premise of one all-powerful, all-wise, ever-present God who is primarily concerned with humankind's well-being. In particular, it violates Muhammad's stringent requirement that no other god can be nor ever should be associated with Allah. Yet Islam has Iblis, authorized by Allah to exercise what appears to be virtually god-like though malevolent powers until the Day of Judgment, when the world will come to an end and Iblis will be assigned to perdition.

In the minds of most Muslims, especially the more superstitious among them, Iblis in turn associates with himself a formidable host of evil spirits: ifrits, djinn, and other malevolent attendants, many of whom can, however, be propitiated and may even be helpful in small ways. In Islamic Morocco there are also semideities, sidi (saints who possess healing powers, a role comparable to some saints in the Roman Catholic religion).

In Roman Catholicism, one finds both God and Satan, each surrounded by an innumerable retinue: angels, or infernal agents, arranged in a sort of hierarchy. One finds also the curious but powerful Cult of the Virgin Mary, a sort of religion within a religion. God is held to be supreme, but the technical distinction between monotheism and polytheism here devolves into theological quibble.

Deus Universalis is manifest in all being; Deus Sapiens in the soul of human beings. As people are the product of the dynamism of the universe, so the deities of their perceptions may be said to have the same origin and ultimate validity. So long as people exist, Deus Sapiens is an entity essential to their well-being as individuals and social animals. It is an entity worthy of the highest efforts of the best students of psychology, working independently or in collaboration with those theologians who can put aside their preoccupation with outmoded mythology and their respective scaffoldings of theological doctrines, creeds, and dogma.

While human beings can hardly relate in a personal emotional way to Deus Universalis, they have made much effort to relate intellectually and in practical ways through a growing knowledge of natural laws and their applications. We have seen how a wise doctor provides medicines and proper environmental conditions whereby the natural vitality of an ailing patient is enabled to throw off the effects of the disease or injury from which he might otherwise have died. Psychological factors involving as yet little understood changes in neuronal activity in the brain (psychosomatic medicine) may play a large part in this process, and the wise doctor will have enlisted this factor as fully as possible in his treatment. The better informed and more resourceful the doctor, the more likely that he will be able to change the odds in favor of the patient's survival and whole recovery. His power to do so may be described as a "worshipful experience" vis-à-vis Deus Universalis. Simply to be thankful one is alive, or thankful for pleasant thoughts and feelings is to have a worshipful relationship with Deus Universalis. One who is not thankful is nevertheless having a relationship—of a different kind—with Deus Universalis. The relationship cannot be avoided.

This capability of the human mind and the options that it opens up are our species' special privilege and responsibility. Here lies the power and potential of Deus Sapiens, derived from Deus Universalis. When an individual voluntarily exercises what power he has over his mind to bring out its highest potential—for example, to create beautiful art, to induce some variety of transcendental or mystical religious experience, or to relate to fellow man in an act of generosity and compassion—that action is a manifestation of Deus Sapiens and the highest sort of "worshipful experience" vis-à-vis Deus Universalis (Deus Sapiens, being derived from the latter).

We must examine further the proposition that peoples' religious feelings, which are important here because their effects on human actions—whether beneficent or the opposite—are in reality physiological phenomena, involving the responses and interaction of certain neurons (brain cells) in the presence of various stimulators and inhibitors. Poets tend to speak of such matters as divine mystery; realists' position must be that this phenomenon is indeed "divine" insofar as the all-encompassing dynamism, which we have identified as Deus Universalis, did in the course of cosmic time produce a creature generically endowed with the special kind of cells specially arranged and provided with necessary reagents, linkages, (neurons, neurotransmitters, central nervous system, and all the rest) that have the potential, and indeed provide a compulsion to bring about the special religious thoughts and feelings that shape human actions and differentiate *Homo sapiens* from other animals. It is indeed a "mysterious" phenomenon inasmuch as human beings, despite their special intellectual equipment, cannot yet (and perhaps never will) fully understand and control it.

It is redundant to recite the evidence of people's unique religious nature. One finds it in archaeological digs as prehistoric shrines and altars, in countless temples, churches, mosques, monuments of every size and description representing diverse levels of cultural advancement, in written records, in music, poetry, painting, sculpture, and in the institutions created to carry out religious and charitable objectives.

To say that this generic quality, inherent in the condition of being human, is unequally distributed and unequally cultivated among individuals and social groups adds nothing to what we already know about other heritable characteristics and abilities. In part this would be due to the individual's actual physiological inheritance: the number and type of neurons and other physical aspects of brain and central nervous system. In modern computer terminology, this would be called the design and quality of the "hardware."

More important would be the "software"—the individual's early childhood experiences, his or her feelings of being wanted or unwanted, peer culture, and all the other subtle and complex influences that contribute to the "preprogramming" of the human brain in all its aspects, religious nature or psyche being only one. In addition to this involuntary programming are other "programs" that the individual may enter into his or her computer-brain voluntarily. Finally, there is the choice of uses to which the operator may elect to devote this complex machinery and the range of opportunities available.

Great thinkers of history would have been great thinkers at any time in any culture. Aristotle's contribution, for example, would be very great but probably would be quite different if he were alive today. Einstein's intellectual gifts would have made a contribution to any advanced society in which he found himself, but certainly would have been different had he lived, for example, in ancient Greece or China. However, we must not omit to mention the hostility that great genius can arouse among people not ready for nor attuned to its output.

The concept of Deus Sapiens seems, superficially at least, more or less synonymous with the human soul. In a larger sense, it is the summation of forces arising out of human beings' unique mental endowments delineated above. The word "soul" must be carefully defined, or avoided. It is unfortunately one of those words, like "love" and "faith," which mean many different things to different people, and different things to the same person when used in different contexts. The Greek word psyche is perhaps more specific. Yet "the science of the psyche," psychology, deals rather too broadly with an individual's reactions to his environment in general. Psychology is defined as the science or study of the activities of living things and their interaction with the environment. Elements contributed to human beings' behavior by their religious nature, or their souls—if recognized at all—are merely incidental. The medical discipline of psychiatry deals primarily with mental disorders.

Taking a cue from William James, we seek, however, to broaden his definition of "religious experience," and show it to be a physiologically normal, healthy, instinctive quality, genetically inherent in human beings, a denominator common to all humankind, manifested in many diverse religious formulations, but unfortunately capable of doing harm as well as good.

We believe that human beings' religious nature (Deus Sapiens) is a quality that gives rise to moral behavior yet is not itself a code of morals—a quality that seeks to help relieve others' pain and suffering (utilizing perhaps medical and psychiatric knowledge or even yoga lore to that end), but is not itself a mere body of medical knowledge. It is a quality imbued with love, goodwill, forgiveness, and compassion, asking nothing in return yet not to be exploited as merely "schmoo" or "patsy." At its best and most effective, it is a quality acting as a magnet to polarize, or like yeast to leaven, or charisma to inspire one's self and other people toward the well-being of humankind.

When directed toward the well-being of humankind, and only then, this special quality, unique to humankind, may be equated with the terms "Holy Spirit" or "Logos."[1] The former term is used in the three synoptic Gospels, the latter by the writer of the Gospel according to John (who also uses Holy Spirit) and by other early Christian writers. Somewhat the same things might be said equally, we believe, of the spirit and source of guidance recognized by other religions—though their objectives might be personal perfection rather than the well-being of all humankind. Buddhism in particular would have its own Pali or Sanskrit word (Karma?), and Sufism its own Arabic word to convey the same or a closely similar concept. Arabic, for example, has several root words that may be translated as "to be rightly guided." Often in context, however, they seem to imply merely the superficial observance of rules for conduct set forth in the Quran.

Sufism, in most of its many manifestations, is aimed at a more direct emotional experience of the spirit of God than mere conformity to rules, set forth in the Quran. In this respect it seems to parallel Christ's attempted reformation of Judaism. In both cases, that is, Sufis on the one hand and those who followed Christ's own teachings closely on the other, some sought their goal in personal, mystic escape experiences and others by ministering to the sick, poor, and oppressed. The two routes—mysticism and social service—are not necessarily mutually exclusive, though their social impact is quite different.

In the scenario followed by this work, the effect of the Holy Spirit, Logos, Karma (?), their Arabic equivalents, and equivalents in any other language, would be found at the very highest end of the spectrum or hypothetical bell curve established by analysis of men's religious natures. It may shine forth in the lives of people who profess no religious affiliation as well as in the lives of devoted followers of various recognized religious sects. It is a universal human quality, though its manifestation may be frustratingly rare. It is not proprietary to any sect or cult.

In a definition of terms, Deus Sapiens is all-inclusive: covers the entire spectrum or bell curve referred to above. The "Deus" part is a collective for all the diverse gods and spirits whom people have worshipped and all the diverse theological formulations that they have constructed, including some that now appear as sheer nonsense. The term Holy Spirit or Logos, or whatever equivalent there may be in any other language, refers to a central nucleus or core (comparable perhaps to the compass of a navigating system and, at the same time, the energy unit in a power-generating system). As a matter of definition its function is purely beneficent and never negative or harmful. We hold that this "core" is a genetic heritage in the human species, however recessive it may seem.

The fact that human beings have based the many and varied religious systems that they have formulated upon premises quite incompatible with evidence provided by scientific observation and reasoning does not invalidate the reality of and necessity for Deus Sapiens, but simply calls for a reexamination of the *perceptions* of that force engendered by human beings. In many cases, apparent aberrations have provided valuable benefits to humankind, which one would wish to preserve. The wise psychiatrist, as he administers to the needs of his patients does not scoff at nor seek immediately to destroy their delusions, but rather enters into the strange worlds they have created, hoping to be able to introduce concepts that will eventually lead each patient to more rational views.

We turn our attention first to the belief in life after death, which sometimes presumes a literal resurrection of the body and in other cases calls for its continuation in a nonmaterial spiritual form, adhering more or less closely to the personal characteristics and life-style of the deceased. All evidence gathered through scientific observations and the application of common sense, relegates the once-prevalent belief in resurrection of the body, to an offensive absurdity. Yet, the resurrection-of-the-body idea remains embedded in the official Nicene and Apostles creeds, and in the funeral services of many churches. It is central to the beliefs of Islam. Among more educated people it has become a matter of no importance; but no one has the heart nor any particular incentive to dispel what to some may be a comforting illusion. It may be harmless nonsense from one point of view perhaps, but it is a string for the bow of retrogressive theology.

It will reward our time to examine briefly the history of belief in a future life. Such belief formed a very important part of Egyptian court life and religious ritual from earliest times, though possibly the hope and privilege only of the ruling classes, not for the common people. The early Jewish patriarch Abraham, who would have been familiar with Egyptian ways, demonstrated great concern for the proper burial of his half-sister and wife, Sarah, but other members of his large entourage evoked no such concern. Nothing was said about future life. Later Jews had their Sheol, a place where the dead passed a dreary and interminable existence. The idea of release and passing on to bliss or torment appears in Hebrew writings of the Babylonian Captivity period, but never assumed much importance in Jewish cosmology.

The hope and expectation of a future life was given top priority as a result of Christ's death and resurrection. This was consistent with Christ's ministry primarily to the poor and outcast, bringing hope to the hopeless and relief to those in suffering. Christ himself obviously believed in a second coming (whose nature is obscure) and held out hope to his followers that they would dwell with the heavenly father in a "house of many mansions." This Christian scenario would offer hope, and indeed positive assurance of a blessed life in the after-world, a very great benefaction to those oppressed in this life, for example, to slaves in their hopeless misery, to those in prison, to martyrs in their hour of trial, and to wealthy housewives in their boredom.

Muhammad later took up the idea of a future life and made it one of the central articles of faith in Islam—the religion of "surrender" to the will of God (Allah) in this world, but with absolute assurance of a future Day of Judgment. On the right hand (though Allah himself has no hands as such) is an eternal paradise of beautiful fields, running water, lovely damsels ever young, and all that a desert people could want, and on the left hand a fiery pit with all the torments they could imagine.

The kingdom of heaven, or of God, so frequently mentioned in the Gospels, has been taken as primarily a blueprint for a future life. However that may be, it was *not* just for a future life, but a pattern of life for the living: real, here and now—a blueprint for life on Earth. Christ admonished his followers to pray:

> Thy kingdom come,
> Thy will be done
> *On Earth* as it is in heaven. . . .

(author's italics)

and again, in Luke (17:20–21):

The Pharisees asked him, "When will the kingdom of God come?" He said, "You cannot tell by observation when the kingdom of God comes. There will be no saying, "Look, here it is! or 'There it is!'; for in fact the kingdom of God is among you."

(Note that the last line can also be translated:
". . . is within you.")

This "kingdom" of God or heaven, incidentally was not in any way threatening to Caesar's Empire, but symbiotic, even synergetic. It could not exist except under the umbrella of a strong central government; it had no army or civil bureaucracy, and its members would be peace-loving, helpful, obedient to all lawful orders, would walk the extra mile, turn the other cheek, and so on. He said: "Render unto Caesar the things that are Caesar's, and unto God the things that are God's."

Muhammad made an even more important feature of Islam's belief in a future life and the Day of Judgment. The Quran promises and frequently reiterates the promise of a future life with eternal youth and all the pleasures thereof, especially to those who die fighting for the faith, but also to others who keep the law, offset by a promise of every imaginable torment to unbelievers and sinners— "companions of the right" and "of the left," respectively—the carrot-and-stick syndrome. This inducement made every soldier lost in battle a "martyr" for the faith and resulted in recklessly brave armies. It enabled the famous medieval religious order of Assassins to function as it did. Even today, though more conservative Muslims are probably somewhat skeptical, it has produced unnumbered young "martyrs" in the Iran-Iraq War and the car-bomb suicide terrorists of Lebanon and elsewhere.

However, even within Islam, other voices arose. Omar Khayyam, brilliant mathematician, poet, and sometime Sufi, wrote (ca. A.D. 1100):[2]

> Oh, threats of Hell and Hopes of Paradise!
> One thing at least is certain—*This* Life flies.
>   One thing is certain and the rest is Lies;
> The Flower that once has blown forever dies.
>
> Strange is it not? that of the myriads who
> Before us pass'd the door of Darkness through,
>   Not one returns to tell us of the Road,
> Which to discover we must travel too.
>
> I sent my Soul through the invisible,
> Some letter of that After-life to spell;
>   And by and by my Soul returned to me,
> And answer'd, "I myself am Heav'n and Hell:
>
> Heav'n but the vision of fulfill'd Desire,
> And Hell the shadow from a Soul on fire,
>   Cast on the Darkness into which Ourselves,
> So late emerged from, shall so soon expire."

(Fitzgerald translation)

Belief in a future life has given hope and strength to the hopeless for two millenia. Hope of heaven and/or fear of hell, which we now label pure superstition, has doubtless exercised a powerful influence on the behavior of many individuals. Certainly that hope and fear have provided a source of revenue to all manner of religious establishments. One thinks of the temples and tombs of ancient Egypt; of the votive paintings in the Buddhist eighth to tenth century rock-cut caves at Tun-Huang in western China, terminus of one of the major silk routes; of the lovely Romanesque churches in France along the several pilgrim routes leading to Santiago de Compostela; and indeed of every great synagogue, temple, church, or mosque, and of the gifts, endowments, waqfs, and other sources of revenue needed to support them. One thinks less pleasantly of the medieval Catholic Church's sale of indulgences to the ignorant and superstitious, especially by the Papal agent Tetzel, whose excesses provided the spark to ignite Luther's Reformation movement.

The mentality out of which the medieval system of indulgences developed is still active in the dogma that only by an act of repentance can one achieve "salvation"—meaning as a practical matter, admission to heaven. The fact that one could confess, repent, and be saved *in extremis*, or any time, or many times, took the teeth out of the aforementioned fear of hell. Indeed it invited the cynical to sin if for no other reason than in order to establish a base from which to be saved, or a St. Augustine to say: "Lord make me good, but not just yet!"

Official Christian theology holds that everyone is a sinner, that just being born couldn't happen without sin (and to be sure, a latent sense of guilt about sex and many other matters is a natural and very widespread human psychological characteristic). Thus, many Presbyterian Church services spend the first few minutes reminding the congregation what terrible sinners they are (a message that only the most saintly really believe). This is followed by a message of great joy: Christ died for your sins; accept him and you are saved!

There is the story of the grasping and miserly laird who lived in a poor farming community somewhere in Scotland. In all his life he had visited the local kirk only a half-dozen times, for weddings or funerals, and had given little or nothing toward church expenses. Finally as he felt his end approaching, he called in the impoverished rector and asked, "Sandy, if I gie ye fifty punds, will I go to heaven?" Sandy was wrestling with his conscience, and as he wrestled the laird upped the ante, "a hundred punds?" Sandy still wrestled, and the laird got up to 500 pounds, an enormous sum in that community. Sandy could stand it no longer, "I canna say, but t'will be a verra guid expurriment!"

On the other hand, one thinks of ultraorthodox Jewish sects

whose members spend their entire lives as a ritual to be carried out in accordance with the innumerable details of Mosaic Law, studying and arguing about Torah, Mischna, Midrash, and Talmud, supplemented by vigorous correspondence regarding matters of behavior not exactly covered by any of those authorities, or where authorities are in conflict. As noted above, Judaism appears more world-centered and less heaven-centered than Christianity and Islam; life itself is a complex ritual, to be gotten through in accordance with the Law, for reasons not entirely clear, apparently *not* primarily in hopes of a better deal in a future life.

Observance of ritual is, to be sure, an important prop for the human psyche. From the navy seaman who salutes an empty quarter-deck when he comes abroad ship late at night and the ritual-obsessed Orthodox Jews mentioned above to the most "liberated" modernist, everybody has some sort of cherished ritual. Nearly every religious sect or cult makes important use of ritual to induce or enhance the spirit of worship, and it is a very important element also in many secular relationships. Witness, for example, the best-seller popularity of books on etiquette by Emily Post, Cleveland Amory, and their like.

To the earliest Jews, sin and guilt, and repentance and atonement were national rather than personal concerns. All were involved, but the leaders (first Moses, then the judges, then the kings) were intermediaries between God and the people. The Jews' special God had revealed to Moses (and to anonymous scribes centuries later who attributed revelations to him) the rules for conduct, and had spelled out very precisely the rituals that they, his special people, were to perform. God was "up there" but never far away. He might overlook a few slip-ups, but one never could be sure. When he was pleased, the nation prospered. When he was angry, he used drought or plague or military defeat to chastise them as a wise father would chastise an erring son.

Under Moses (ca. 1250 B.C.) the nation was formed. Under the judges (until ca. 1060 B.C.) it seemed to be floundering. Then under Kings David (d. 973 B.C.) and Solomon (d. 933 B.C.), the Lord showed His pleasure and approbation, and Israel reached its halcyon days. After that, however, things seemed never to go very well for very long for the Jewish nation. They sinned and their prophets scolded them. They struggled unsuccessfully to get back into God's favor and never gave up trying. By the time of the Babylonian Captivity, however, the idea had been introduced that the individual could have a meaningful relationship with God (could win His favor if he would repent and atone) even though God still turned His face away from the Jews as a nation. Having a humble and contrite heart was important, but strict technical observance of the Law, and performance of prescribed ritual were even more basic to a satisfactory relationship with God.

The message proclaimed by Jesus of Nazareth and the reform that he sought to bring about in Judaism was simply a reversal of this emphasis. He stressed the idea that, without abrogating the Law, the humble and contrite heart or, perhaps better, a compassionate, forgiving, understanding heart, was more important than the Law. Holy Spirit rather than the dictates of priests and doctors of Law was the proper go-between from God to man.

Islam (A.D. 622) provided an even more direct relationship between God and people, there is no priesthood (but also no recognition of the Holy Spirit or Logos, as we have defined it).[3] The relationship between God and human beings is still based on strict adherence to rules and rituals set forth in the Quran. Very soon after the Prophet's death (A.D. 632), the Sufi movement grew up within Islam, emphasizing direct mystical relationship to God. This idea, which arguably is rather close to the Holy Spirit/Logos idea, was regarded as heretical until the time of al-Ghazali, at about A.D. 1100. The history of the Sufi movement is a separate study, providing examples of very high and selfless spiritual development and also examples of exploitation, ignorance, superstition. Some (but certainly not all) of the Sufis in medieval times seemed rather closer to Christ's original position than most (but certainly not all) of the nominal Christians of that time.

It is the position of this book, of course, that there can be no sapient (which is to say anthropomorphic) being "up there" in the absence of an actual human brain. There can be no brain without special molecules arranged into neurons with all their complex interrelationships, plus the neurotransmitters and all that goes to make up the human central nervous system. There is indeed the infinitely vast, impersonal, impartial, ever-active energy of the universe (Deus Universalis), the creator and essence of all matter in every form and which imparts to that matter whatever dynamism it may manifest, including of course the above-mentioned most remarkably dynamic assemblage of molecules, the human brain. This abstract energy activates but does not guide the workings of the human brain.

Quite clearly some arrangement or some special quality imparted to special neurons within that brain, arrived at accidentally perhaps in the course of some mutation (thus, as one may say, "created" by Deus Universalis) produces a strong proclivity for it to operate in its own best interest and in what it perceives as the best interest of those close and dear to that individual human being. "Best interest" here encompasses basic survival and gratification of various instincts that mark human beings as predators little removed from fellow animals. However, human beings, unlike other animals, are redeemed (or condemned to suffer guilt) by being predators with a conscience and with compassion—qualities associated closely with their upward-reaching souls, and intellectual and cultural aspirations.

The sum total of these elements—from the proclivity to temper aggression in accordance with dictates of conscience and compassion, and to harbor concern for the well-being of all humankind (roughly, the Holy Spirit or Logos), to the creation of all sorts of gods, good spirits, bad spirits, and the theological formulations that go with them—produces the rather untidy conglomerate that we are calling, for convenience's sake, Deus Sapiens. Deus Sapiens is therefore derived from and completely dependent on Deus Universalis; yet, in one special limited respect, it may be said to be a more powerful and effective force in human affairs. It not only provides the human touch, but also incorporates the deified capacities of the human brain for analysis, conceptualizing, and planning.

Finally, we turn attention to an examination of the premises and efficacy of prayer—another of the long-established manifestations of *Homo sapiens'* religious nature. There are many kinds of prayer. All presume the existence of a power or being somewhere "out there," who may or may not listen and may or may not respond. The being may be propitiated if he is angry, and if in a good mood he may do something specific to help specific people. The suppliant is reassured if he can feel that God looks on him with favor. This feeling of assurance on the individual's part is a self-generated state of mind within the human suppliant. Prayer may also help the suppliant to straighten things out in his or her own mind. Sometimes God's role in prayer is simply as a silent recipient of emotional outbursts of joy, grief, thanks, exasperation, repentance, or whatever.

There are many ways of praying, all of which give man some real satisfaction or he wouldn't do it. One thinks of illiterate monks in Tibet or Nepal endlessly turning prayer wheels containing prayers written in letters they cannot understand, presumably in hope that the divine entity or some attendant spirit will read. One thinks also of the many examples of answered prayer attested to by fundamentalist and evangelical-type Christians. One family, traveling by rail in rural India from one mission station to another under circumstances of urgency, reached a lonely junction late at night, too late to make an all-important connection. What would they do? There was no place to go. The next train would not be along until late next day. Not knowing what else to do, they got down on their knees right there on the station platform and placed their problem in the hands of the Lord. Lo! in a matter of minutes, an unscheduled "extra" came puffing in, going their way, and off they went!

One thinks of the Baptist minister who was refused permission to deliver the eulogy for a long-time friend and colleague, a prominent Episcopalian minister whose funeral service attracted widespread attention. Episcopalian services don't have eulogies. He was, however, to be called upon for a prayer. When called upon, and some say for 40 minutes thereafter, he poured out to the Lord in the eloquence for which he was noted, his own gratitude and the thanks of all the people of that great city for all the wonderful qualities possessed by the deceased and for all the wonderful good works that he had done. One cannot question but that the Lord was edified, and the family of the deceased were pleased to have had the privilege of hearing that prayer.

One thinks of public gatherings where opening and closing prayers seem designed to tell the Lord what is needed, how to do it, and even to sign Him up as sponsor for the cause being promoted.

One thinks, of course, of the parable of the widow's mite: the vainglorious ostentatious prayer of the wealthy Pharisee loudly dedicating a munificient sum to the service of the Lord and thanking the Lord for how good he (the Pharisee) was, contrasted with the silent humble prayer of the widow who had quietly given all she had. The moral is plain, yet anyone who has struggled to raise "big bucks" for worthy causes must have quietly offered his or her own prayer for "leadership giving" by as many wealthy Pharisees as can be persuaded to do it.

During World War I Christian churches in America and in Germany were simultaneously (with allowance for time difference) offering prayers to the Lord to give victory to the troops representing their side.

Perhaps the point has been made. Prayer serves a universal need of humankind, a need that must and will be met, a need as universal as the innate religious nature that became part of human beings' genetic makeup by virtue of the mutation or mutations that have distinguished them from other animals.

The diverse images that human beings have formulated to provide the necessary counterfoil to this universal human need are a tribute to human ingenuity. Among humans the need is real and therefore a scientific fact. The images they create are *to them* real, but cannot be corroborated by scientific observation. Science has not come forward with any alternative formulation that will satisfactorily meet such a need and can scarcely be expected to do so. As we have characterized the need to believe in a future life as a string to the bow of retrogressive theology, so we must characterize the need for prayer as a quiver of arrows.

Beyond that, some people believe implicitly in an actual physical force at work, which if confirmed would provide substance to man's faith in the power of prayer to help others in distress or to fill personal needs. They seem to hold in effect that prayer may create "vibrations" of a type under examination through various quasi-scientific parapsychological investigations, vibrations that can evoke positive physical responses in other specially sensitive brains that are attuned to that wave band, sometimes over very long distances. We have already noted the possibility of extrasensory communication among humans and even among animals. Innumerable examples of the power of prayers are cited as miracles that really happened.

One interrupts one's self to recall the patriarchal pronouncement of the great physicist, I. I. Rabi: "There is no such thing as a miracle; only happenings that we don't understand." Yet such phenomena cannot be dismissed. If these things really happen, it is either random chance or there must be a physiological reason for them. The capabilities of the human brain are almost completely unknown and may conceivably include the capacity to send and receive such "vibrations."

NOTES

1. We use the terms "Holy Spirit" and "Logos" as virtually interchangeable, and venture to characterize that aspect of human religious nature to

which they refer as a combined guidance system and action motivator. Another very similar term would be "inner light," which is central to Quaker belief. Traditionally this originates with God and is "beamed in" on humankind in general, but is picked up more particularly by a relatively few individuals—men and women specially gifted with receivers tuned to that particular wave band. Simply to receive these (as it were) "radio waves" is not enough; the receiver set should be able to filter out all static and should be able to amplify the resultant broadcast so that others may hear too.

We believe that all the scientific evidence assembled so far suggests nothing more radical than a new perception as to the location of the transmitter. Instead of coming from a broadcasting station somewhere "up there," it comes from somewhere "in here." The voice heard is not that of a disembodied spirit, "God-up-there," but the functioning of a certain unimaginably complex special arrangement of neurons, "God-in-here." Comparison with the radar principle, which we have already introduced, is more apt than comparison with separate radio stations, one to broadcast and one to receive, each manned by different persons.

We would hold, though the point is arguable, that the Holy Spirit/Logos concept identifies only a very narrow wave band in the broad spectrum of wave bands allegedly utilized by God to communicate with people, a narrow band that carries only material beneficial to *all* human beings. The argument would arise over questions such as whether *all* human beings refers to an unlimited world population of possibly 10 to 15 billion individuals barely able to eke out a minimum survival subsistence, or to a much smaller number limited by the objective of enabling all to live in robust good health and to achieve the highest intellectual, cultural, and spiritual development to which humankind may reasonably aspire.

The concept of a Holy Spirit can be traced in writings of the Old Testament but was most forcefully set forth by Christ:

> And so I tell you this: no sin, no slander, is beyond forgiveness for man, except slander spoken against the Spirit, and that will not be forgiven. Any man who speaks a word against the Son of Man will be forgiven; but if anyone speaks against the Holy Spirit, for him there is no forgiveness, either in this age or in the age to come.
>
> (Matthew 12:31–32; similarly, Mark 3:28–30)

Later, in Acts and sometimes in Paul's Epistles, the term "holy spirit" (with initials deliberately set in lower case to distinguish the term from the above) refers to the force that caused congregations to undergo seizures, to speak in tongues or exhibit other bizarre behavior. *Hastings Dictionary of the Bible* (Grant and Rowley, 1963) carries a long and scholarly article on this subject, starting with a definition that is decidedly lower case from our point of view:

> HOLY SPIRIT—The mysterious creative power of God, possessing and inspiring men, manifested especially in ecstatic conditions, prophesying, and special abilities such as strength, leadership, wisdom, judgment and skill; sometimes conceived as a quasi-physical force impelling its recipient somewhat in the manner of the wind setting in motion the dust of the ground, but coming to be recognized as the personal activity of God Himself.

The article proceeds to trace the use of the term and the development of the concept in the Old Testament, in extracanonical writings, and in the New Testament. We return to a discussion of Holy Spirit (initials capitalized) as we believe Christ intended it, which is compatible to our faith in the existence of an innate quality in the human psyche, which guides and motivates us in our exertions toward an optimum and maximum, physical and spiritual well-being for humankind.

The term Logos as an exact or approximate equivalent to Holy Spirit was introduced into biblical usage by the writer of the Gospel according to John. This was the latest of the Gospels, having been completed, it is now thought, around A.D. 90–110. A date of A.D. 65–70 is favored for Mark, the earliest of the Gospels, and the other synoptic Gospels not much later. Thus, regardless of content, the style of writing and vocabulary used would be that of a later generation. The use of the word Logos, in particular, with the meaning that we attach to it, is noted in the writings of Justin Martyr (ca. A.D. 100–165) and may be traced to the writings of Philo of Alexandria (ca. 20 B.C.–A.D. 50).

Philo of Alexandria was a Hellenized Jew whose writings are known to have had strong influence on early church fathers, including St. Paul. Although himself a Jew and active on behalf of the Jewish colony in Alexandria, Philo's writing seems intended as much or more for Greco-Roman audiences, with the objective of bringing about a better understanding of Judaism. It should be remembered that Judaism went through a phase of vigorous missionary outreach at that time. It was one of several Eastern religions competing with Christianity for the minds and hearts of the Roman population, and was widely adopted. As late as the eighth century, a Jewish missionary persuaded the ruler of the Khazar nation (a Turkic tribe that controlled the lower Volga River region) to adopt Judaism as the official religion for his nation, rather than the Christianity of Byzantium or Islam of the Arabs (the two world powers at that time). The only fragments of Philo's writings that have been preserved are those quoted in the writings of early church fathers.

Christ himself would not have known of Philo or his writings, and the writers of the synoptic Gospels either did not know or had no reason to introduce a new word where Christ had used a perfectly serviceable one. The writer of John, whose whole approach is markedly different from the other three, was writing for a later audience for whom the word Logos would have carried special meaning.

The Holy Spirit/Logos concept was, by general agreement, most perfectly exemplified in the life of Jesus of Nazareth. It may be seen in many other lives, notably those of Buddha and St. Francis of Assisi, but also in unnumbered lives of less influential, less remembered persons. Jesus's life in particular seems to have been taken from the realm of reality into a world of theological fiction to support the doctrinal premises of what became the established orthodox church. Therefore, it is well to start over (at square one, so to speak) and review from the perspective of an unprecommitted inquiring historian what can be learned from a rereading of the Gospel records.

There are two versions of the nativity story: Matthew's and Luke's. Both affirm the myth of virgin birth, which tells us that the myth was introduced sometime after Christ's death (ca. 33) but before the writing of the earliest Gospel (ca. 65–70). The possibility of later alterations to the Gospels cannot be entirely ruled out.

During his lifetime, Christ had been regarded by his companions and contemporaries as the natural son of Joseph and Mary. Any claim to be the promised Christ, the Messiah of the scriptures ("Christ" is simply the Greek translation of "messiah"), would depend on his descent in the male line from King David, son of Jesse. Both Matthew and Luke meticulously provide records of such descent showing that Joseph was indeed descended from David. The fact that their records do not agree does not negate the fact that both writers thought it necessary to establish the connection. As the period from death of David to the birth of Jesus was about 975 years, the blood, or genes of David would have been widely disseminated throughout Judah by that time.

Luke (3:23) begins his lineage: "The son, as people thought, . . ." This tells us two things: (1) That is what they did think, and indeed it is evident from many other passages that the parents thought so too, and (2) Somebody at a later time had introduced a different thought. One translation of Matthew's lineage (1:7–16, cited in *The New English Translation*) reads: "David was the father of Solomon . . . the father of Joseph and Joseph, to whom Mary, a virgin, was betrothed, was the father of Jesus." *Hastings Dictionary of the Bible* points out that the Hebrew word, here translated as virgin, simply meant an unmarried girl. Virginity in our understanding of that word was an extremely important qualification under Jewish ethos for a first-time bride, but the Hebrew word used here could be applied equally well to a young widow.

Supporting our contention, that both Joseph and Mary thought of Jesus as their child, Luke's nativity account goes on to say that it was *the parents* who "brought the child Jesus to the temple to do for him what was customary under the Law. . . . The child's father and mother were full of wonder at what was being said about him" (author's italics). Later in the same chapter of Luke, one finds the well-known story of the visit to the temple when Jesus was 12 years old. He had stayed behind to talk with the elders and teachers. His distraught parents "returned to Jerusalem to look for him; and after three days they found him. . . . His *parents* were astonished to see him there, and his mother said to him, 'My son, why have you treated us like this? Your father and I have been searching for you in great anxiety'."

Jesus's reply on that occasion was "'Did you not know that I was bound to be in my Father's house?' But they did not understand what he meant." Their failure to understand introduces a duality that prevails throughout the Gospels and has not been resolved satisfactorily to this day. Jesus refers to himself or is referred to roughly half the time as the Son of Man and half as the Son of God.

We hold (with all reverence and respect) that he was a normal human being in the medical sense of the term, however especially gifted he may have been in the intellectual and spiritual sense. He did, even at the age of 12, obviously envision a new relationship with the Supreme Being which became the substance of his ministry. It was perhaps a tribute, and if so one of the most beautiful tributes of all time, to the firm kindliness, wisdom, protection, and support he had experienced at the hands of his father, Joseph, that he chose the father-child relationship to convey to the people of his time his meaning about the ideal relationship between themselves and God, the heavenly father. Later, speaking of little children (3 to 7 years old, we would imagine), he said, "The kingdom of God belongs to such as these. I tell you, whoever does not accept the kingdom of God like a child will never enter it" (Mark 10:15–16).

Once his mother and brothers had come seeking him and found him speaking in the midst of a crowd; he responded to their messenger, "Who is my mother? Who are my brothers? . . . Whoever does the will of my heavenly Father is my brother, my sister, my mother." All believers are equally children of the same Father in that sense, Jesus included. He is simply the one who knows the way and feels called upon to show others. The Lord's Prayer is to be addressed, not to Christ's special Father, but to the Father of all, to our Father in heaven. This use of the word Father establishes the nature of the relationship to the heavenly spirit and in no way repudiates the physiological fact that all people also have human fathers as a necessary precondition to their having been born.

To the inquiring historian, the most probable scenario to account for the introduction of the literal virgin-birth-fatherhood-of-God myth would start with the fact that Christ's reform movement (having been totally rejected by mainline Judaism) found a ready response in the Greco-Roman world. Greatness among heroes of Greek mythology was accounted for by their having been born of the union between a mortal and a god or goddess. For example, Hercules, the greatest of the Greco-Roman heroes, was one of nonidentical twins. His remarkable strength was attributed to the somewhat implausible story that Zeus/Jupiter had first changed himself into the likeness of Amphitryon, Alcmene's husband, and had taken her into his arms; then later that same night, Amphitryon himself had returned from doing battle somewhere and had come to her bed. Thus, Hercules and his twin Iphicles, were presumed to be half-brothers: Hercules the Son of Zeus and Iphicles the son of Amphitryon.

Hercules's mythological career had certain parallels to Christ's (as well as many extreme differences). He performed miracles (of strength). He suffered greatly, pursued by the vengeance of Juno out of jealousy over her husband's infidelity. He died a horrible death and then was taken up to the Olympian heaven, there to be forgiven by Hera/Juno and united in marriage to her and Zeus/Jupiter's own daughter Hebe, goddess of eternal youth, and presumably to live happily ever after.

One may speculate whether early missionaries seized upon this myth and exploited its similarities to explain Christ's career in terms their hearers would understand, or whether the new non-Jewish congregations, after conversion to Christianity, grafted their own prototype explanation for Christ's greatness upon the gospel story (which they may well have received in imperfect versions anyway). Some other explanation may be offered. Where the virgin birth myth came from must remain an open question. Factually, it didn't happen that way!

Less important to history, but of considerable interest to historians, is the task of reconciling Luke's nativity story with Matthew's. The two fit together very nicely except for Luke's representation that Mary and Joseph were in Nazareth at the time of the Annunciation. Historical evidence makes it quite clear that the Holy Family did not arrive in Nazareth until Jesus was at least three to four years old and that the expedition from Nazareth to Jerusalem, during which time a child was born and laid in a manger, did not take place until he was at least 11 and more likely 12 years old. That scenario would fit in with the story of his having visited Jerusalem with his parents and remained behind at the temple, recited above.

Both writers agree that he was born during the reign of Herod the Great (d. March–April 4 B.C.). Both agree that Mary, after she received the Annunciation, immediately went to see her kinswoman Elizabeth, who was already pregnant with John (later John the Baptist). Matthew says that Mary and Joseph at that time lived in Bethlehem; Luke says in Nazareth. Elizabeth on the other hand must have lived close to Jerusalem as her husband was liable to be called to perform priestly duties there. Jerusalem itself is not over three or four miles from Bethlehem; Nazareth is at least 60 miles away, and farther by the only road, which would lead through rough and dangerous Samaria.

Under Matthew's version, one would have to assume that Jesus was born in Joseph and Mary's house in Bethlehem. It would have been an easy matter for them to accomplish all the ceremonial requirements for a firstborn son, the details of which are so beautifully set forth in Luke's account of the presentation at the temple in Jerusalem. Later, the Magi, wise men from the East, found Jesus in Bethlehem *in his parents' house* (and not in a manger)—(Matthew 2:11–12; author's italics).

Herod in his later years suffered from some horrible and painful malady and was obsessed with anxiety that the succession to his throne would go to someone in his own family—someone of his own choosing; history records that he was ruthless and bloody in the measures he took to ensure that result. There is no record of any visit of Magi nor of the subsequent slaughter of all male children in Bethlehem up to the age of two, but such an event would be a natural fit in the history of those years. The report confirms that the Holy Family lived at that time in Bethlehem not in Nazareth. The event itself could not have occurred later than 5 B.C., and the inclusion of all males up to age two in Herod's cruel order suggests that Jesus might well have been a year old or older. Thus, his birth date is usually set as 6–7 B.C.

Warned by a dream, Joseph and Mary fled to haven in Egypt. At some later date, which could not have been before 3 B.C., they decided to return to Palestine, but not to the "ethnarcy" of Judea and Samaria, now ruled by Herod's vindictive and erratic son Archelaus. Instead, they went to Galilee, a separate jurisdiction ruled by his more level-headed brother Antipas. In going there from Egypt they would have had a double reason to avoid the road through Jerusalem: (1) the roughness of the road through rocky hilly country; and (2) fear of Archelaus's inclination to carry out his father's determination to kill a child whom soothsayers had identified as born to be king of the Jews. They would have taken the coastal road through Gaza, and the first significant town they would have come to outside Archelaus's realm, but inside Antipas's, would be Nazareth.

It is very unlikely that the family visited Jerusalem every year during Archelaus's reign for the Passover festival (though Luke says they did), and

if they did they would have left Jesus behind in Nazareth. However, Archelaus's reign became so bad that he was deposed by the Romans in A.D. 6
and sent into exile in the Province of Gaul. At that time Caesar Augustus
ordered that a census be taken. This particular census may have been a sort
of house-cleaning measure to enable the new governor of the area to find out
what he needed to know to rule efficiently and effectively, or it may have
been one in a long series of census-takings held approximately every 14
years throughout the Empire, a procedure inaugurated early in his reign by
Augustus. This particular census was not recorded in Empire annals but
would have fitted into the pattern. It would be a complex and burdensome
undertaking, and if ordered in A.D. 6, the year of Archelaus's banishment, it
could hardly have been implemented until the following year, A.D. 7.
Quirinius (mentioned by Luke) was indeed overall governor of the region at
that time, and there are other references to a census conducted by him.

Luke says that Joseph and his family were required to go to Bethlehem to
be counted because he was of the house of David. We have suggested that a
large segment of the entire Jewish population of Palestine at that time would
have had some connection with the house of David. A better reason would
have been a law such as that still prevailing in Lebanon that every head of
family had to return to the city where he was born. Mary was pregnant
again. It is known that Jesus had, at the time that his ministry began about
20 years later, four brothers whose names are given, and several sisters
(Matthew 13:55). Presumably Mary was required by law to accompany her
husband to be counted. When they got to Bethlehem there would have been
many others returning for the same purpose. Some may have stayed with
friends, some at the small inn, taking all available rooms, and many who
would have camped in the fields nearby. Mary, either because her normal
time had come or because birth had been induced by the rough journey,
needed shelter. She found it in the stable of the inn and the child who was
born was laid in the manger.

The child was not Jesus. If he had been born in 6 B.C., he would now be
11 years old; if in 7 B.C., a year older. Whether he and the other children had
accompanied their parents on this particular trip is not known for sure, but
the story of his lingering on at the temple would fit nicely into this scenario.
People may have gathered to see the newborn baby, as people are apt to do.
Regarding heavenly choirs and similar phenomena, it is sufficient to re-
affirm that such experiences can be very real to the people who actually have
the experience, while others present may not have seen or heard anything.

Puzzled, the historian can only speculate on how such a mix-up could
occur. Merely as one suggested possibility, it may be noted that Luke had
joined the little group of Christians quite some time after Christ's death.
The best scholarly opinion seems to be inclined toward the belief that he

was not himself a Jew by birth and, although he added many helpful facts that enable the historian to tie in biblical events with Roman records and was a very keen and inquiring observer, he did not question things that he was told in accordance with critical methods that would (or at least should) be followed by modern researchers. The people whom he would ask about events in Jesus's life and who had known Jesus personally would be falling back on distant memories. Mary herself, if she was alive at the time, would probably have been in her eighties and might well have lost track as to which of the memorable events in her life directly involved her famous son.

From the age of 12 until Jesus began his ministry a little over 20 years later, no information is available regarding his life. Luke dates the beginning of John the Baptist's ministry very specifically as in the fifteenth year of Tiberius's reign, which is A.D. 28; Jesus's ministry began soon after that. Jesus had obviously been closely in touch with his kinsman John (the Baptist) before their ministries began; each had great affection and admiration for the other. One scenario that seems to work well is that the two had spent a great deal of time together, some of it perhaps with John as visitor in the carpentry shop at Nazareth, more of it probably with Jesus as visitor to John in his strange wilderness habitat. This scenario also fits a general pattern, confirmed certainly in the lives of Moses and Muhammad, of long periods alone and withdrawn from normal social intercourse, when God's message could have been taking shape within the prophets' psyches.

Shortly after his baptism by John, Jesus withdrew into the wilderness again and experienced the well-known temptation by Satan. Of special interest to the historian was the temptation to do homage to Satan and to receive in return dominion over all the kingdoms of the world and the glory that goes with it (Luke 4:5–6). It would have been quite possible for a person of very great ability, charismatic personality, and the gift of leadership to have entered Roman public service and have climbed either the military or the civil service ladder, switching as opportunity offered back and forth from one to the other, arriving quickly at the top. For a person with Jesus's natural gifts that was an open option.

About 15 years after Jesus's birth, a boy was born in one of the Italian hilltowns (to a family no more distinguished than Jesus's) who did just that, and who became the Emperor Vespasian. One may moralize that climbing corporate ladders cannot be done without stepping on other people's fingers and using an occasional body check, but there seems not to have been very much of that in Vespasian's case. To be sure it would be mostly a matter of luck (random chance), or of foul play, to have the right doors open at the right times for the person of great ability to achieve his full potential. Perhaps that is where Satan would come in. In any case Jesus did reject what we may call the Vespasian option.

Two categories of activity in Jesus's career (insofar as we know about it through the Gospels) stand apart from his general teaching. One is his unremitting hostility toward the Pharisees and their allies. The other is his miracles.

The former is so well documented in all the Gospels as to need little review. Matthew 23—the entire chapter is an indictment of Pharisees as bitter as one can read anywhere. Beside it Cicero's famous indictment of Cataline seems mild. The inquiring historian wonders whether he might not have achieved his objective more effectively had he been somewhat more conciliatory. He did say that they (the Pharisees) were unquestioned custodians of the Law—and he had come not to destroy the Law but to perfect it. Evidently "perfecting" was equated in his mind with neutralizing the Pharisees and their allies.

One strains to read into his phrase "to perfect," the broader concept of "reviving and reinvigorating" through introduction of guidance by the Holy Spirit/Logos. He said: "The Sabbath was made for the sake of man and not man for the Sabbath." (To observe the Sabbath was one of the Ten Commandments and therefore a basic requirement in Judaism).

When the Pharisees heard of Jesus's miracles they attributed them to Beelzebub, prince of devils (Matthew 12:24); this accusation evoked his strong statement about the centrality and sanctity of the Holy Spirit (Matthew 12:31-32, quoted on pg. 92).

It was the battle between humanism and fundamentalism that is still going on: those guided by responsive hearts and minds on the one hand, and those guided by the literal words in "The Book" on the other. The truth is that both are needed. All will agree that a society in which every individual is free to go this way and that, guided solely by "inner light" (a Quaker term), would quickly break up in chaos. What we need is "humane fundamentalism" as a basis for law and order.

Finally there are the miracles, closing with the last and greatest: Christ's own death and resurrection. Our puzzlement over Christ's miracles lies in large part in our lack of accurate information as to what really happened in each case. Clearly there was a large component of the sort of faith that he had described as being able to move mountains. That power combined with what we now call as psychosomatic medicine, may well have been enough to effect actual medical cures in many cases and to have changed people's attitudes toward other incurable conditions to the point that what had been debilitating became bearable. How long these cures lasted is another matter; for some a lifetime perhaps—for others, overnight?

The objective of the miracles may have been humanitarian but also to establish the sort of spiritual authority which Moses held. The effect of Christ's miracles seems to have been to astound and delight: to astound those who witnessed them and delight those who benefited by them. None, so far as the record tells us, gave rise to any advance in medical knowledge or improved public health arrangements. No new wine industry sprang up at Cana. We do not have any case histories by which to follow up on events subsequent to the miracle. What happened to the boy whom Christ restored to life as his mother was taking him to the grave? Did he lead a normal healthy productive life and support his mother in her old age? Was he a lifelong invalid who caused her great anxiety and much expense and care? Did he die again the next day?

It may be observed therefore that Christ's miracles, and presumably the rest of his ministry, was directed toward the state of the individual's mind and spirit at the particular moment, then and there. This is the state of mind one finds among young children, again, three to seven, we would guess, who laugh or cry on very short notice and seem to live only for the experience of the moment. He said: ". . . do not be anxious about tomorrow; tomorrow will look after itself. Each day has trouble enough of its own" (Matthew 6:34), and again, ". . . unless you turn round and become like children, you will never enter the kingdom of Heaven." (Matthew 18:3).

We have one glimpse of a momentary overwhelming sense of frustration and anger on Christ's part that his miracles of healing, performed in the villages of Galilee, had not established the sort of unquestioning faith in him and his leadership that Moses's miracles of death and destruction at the Pharaoh's Court had established among the Jews at the time of the Exodus. This observation leads to the further observation that the God in whose name Moses called down his plagues and pestilences upon the Egyptian people was a very withdrawn, terrifying entity, whereas the God of Jesus was kindly, forgiving, and providing—an ever-present father figure.

The circumstances of Christ's own death are clearly drawn. He had made a number of direct or oblique allusions to that coming event during his ministry in the north, before he and his disciples came down to Jerusalem for the high holy days. His unremitting attacks on the Scribes and the Pharisees, on professors of law and their allies, combined with his general popularity among the people, probably angered and possibly scared them. The Gospels tell us that they plotted among themselves how to get rid of him. One has every idea that they would have done so one way or another. The question is only how.

His remarkable action in driving the money changers from the temple grounds during the height of their holy day business invited police action. His silence when arraigned before Pilate on charges of setting up a rival kingdom frustrated what (to this observer at least) seemed a sincere attempt on the part of that fair-minded but politically vulnerable Roman administrator to find grounds upon which to release him. The timetable of these events was such that he would be crucified in the morning of the one day in all the year when bodies must be removed from their crosses and buried before sundown. This was in deference to the Jews' religious sensibilities. In the few cases where figures are given, death on a cross appears to have been a matter of waiting in agony for 36 hours, sometimes longer, before death provided welcome release.

Words do not exist to express one's admiration and awe toward a spirit courageous enough, dedicated to a religious objective with so total and so selfless a dedication as to bring upon himself the suffering and ignominy of death on a cross. After perhaps six hours or so of suffering, Christ proclaimed in a loud voice: "It is finished," and gave up the ghost, as the Bible tells us. Medical people occasionally express a suspicion that he was not yet medically dead. The Roman authorities expressed surprise but on investigation satisfied themselves that it was so. Practitioners of yoga observe that their most advanced practitioners are able to achieve a death-like state of suspended animation by exercise of will power, from which they are restored to life after a time.

The prisoners crucified with Christ were given the coup de grace late in the day but Christ was already dead. A soldier stabbed Christ with his spear but the blade missed vital organs. All bodies were removed from their crosses and buried. Christ was buried under conditions of maximum security.

The most unexplainable part of this "miracle" is how he was enabled to escape those security measures without assistance from some helping hand—of which there is not the slightest suggestion in the record. However that may have been, he was resurrected and did appear among his disciples and followers, greatly enervated, as one might expect, by his terrible experience to the point of not being recognized at first by some. After 40 days, according to Luke's account (Acts 1:3), he died and was buried. Biblical "forty" is not to be taken as an exact count but as equivalent to "a considerable number" (of days, years, or whatever). The report that his body was taken up physically to heaven does not occur in Luke's Gospel, but in Acts. It must be classified as an expression of faith of the mountain-moving variety.

2. None of the following quatrains appear in the Chester Beatty manuscript, which is the earliest known (mid-thirteenth century). Fitzgerald worked from the Oxford codex dated two centuries later (mid-fifteenth century). It is impossible to confirm that all of the nearly 500 quatrains attributed to Omar were in fact written by him.

3. References to Spirit (Arabic: ruh) and/or holy (Arabic: qudus) can be found in the Quran 20 times or more, using the Kassis Concordance. In a

few the meaning comes close to that found in the Bible in passages referring to Mary's conception. An example (Sura 19:17):

> We [meaning Allah] sent to her Our Spirit in the semblance of a full grown man. And when she saw him she said: "May the Merciful defend me from you! If you fear the Lord, leave me and go your way." "I am the messenger of your Lord," he replied, "and have come to give you chaste and without stain a son."

and again (Sura 66:12):

> And in Mary, Imran's daughter, who preserved her chastity and into whose womb We breathed of Our Spirit; who put her trust in the Words of her Lord and his scriptures and was truly devout.

In other places, the meaning may be simply "life," or perhaps "spirituality." For example (Sura 12:25):

> We created man from dry clay, from black molded loam, and before him Satan from smokeless fire. Our Lord said to the angels: "I am creating man from dry clay, from black molded loam. When I have finished him and breathed of My Spirit into him, kneel down and prostrate yourselves before him.

and again (Sura 32:9):

> His first created man from clay, then bred his offspring from a drop of paltry fluid. He molded him and breathed into him of His Spirit. He gave you eyes and ears: yet you are seldom thankful.

Sometimes the Spirit is a messenger; sometimes the thing sent. An example of the latter (Sura 16:2):

> By His will He sends down the angels with the Spirit to those of His servants whom he chooses, bidding them proclaim: "There is no god but Me: therefore fear Me."

Elsewhere, the Spirit appears to be one of the angels (94:4):

> Better is the night of Qudr than a thousand months. On that night the angels and the Spirit by their Lord's leave came down with His decrees.

An example of the Spirit as messenger (Sura 16:102):

> When We [Allah] change one verse for another . . . [men] say: "You [Muhammad] are an impostor." Indeed most of them are ignorant men. Say: "The Holy Spirit brought it down from your Lord in truth to reassure the faithful, and to give guidance and good news to those that surrender themselves to Allah."

and again (Sura 26:193):

> This Book [the Quran] is revealed by the Lord of the Creations. The faithful Spirit brought it down into your heart that you might warn mankind in plain Arabic speech.

Finally, the Holy Spirit does appear as an agency specially given to special people to enable them to do good works (Sura 2:87):

> To Moses We gave the scriptures and after him We sent other apostles. We gave Jesus the son of Mary veritable signs and strengthened him with the Holy Spirit.

and again (Sura 40:15):

> Exalted and enthroned on high, He lets the Spirit descend at His behest on those of his servants whom He chooses, that He may warn them of the day when they shall meet Him: the day when they shall rise up from their graves. . . .

Review of the foregoing does suggest some similarities between the Holy Spirit of the Bible and the Ruh Qudus of Islam as channel of communication between God above—Deus Sapiens—and people here below—*Homo sapiens*. Differences would appear were we to analyze the sorts of messages communicated through that channel conditioned by the differing perceptions of God and the differing circumstances of the particular people.

9 Changing Faces of an Anthropomorphic God

Reiterating the theme of this work, the vast, all-pervasive energy manifest in the big bang and in all matter in every form—from galaxies to the particles that make up the individual atom, and also in all intangible forces of nature—is totally impersonal, impartial, unselective, and uncaring. It operates eternally and unceasingly but without plan or purpose. Our first task is to comprehend that there can be, and is, great consistency and predictability in the manner in which this energy operates at the same time as great unpredictability in the results that follow from its operation. Natural law and random chance are joint partners in the formation of the universe as we know it, and no one can say which is the more important.

The mind of man is one such totally unpredictable result of the joint operation of the natural-law/random-chance partnership. It is hard to imagine that such a complex yet effective machine resulted from a series of random-chance mutations, yet there is no other satisfactory explanation. However, having happened, the existence of human brains marked the introduction of a radically new dimension into the universal scheme of things: an entity capable of comprehending and utilizing for its own purposes some of the many manifestations of that eternal, universal energy; capable also of substituting rational planning for the workings of random chance in many of the happenings that lie within the reach of human beings.

At the same time, the human mind introduced also other new dimensions. It is generically personal, partial, selective, and caring, just the opposite of the force that gave it being and enables it to function. Most importantly, it incorporates a broad spectrum of religious elements along with its other unique capabilities. Out of all these diverse elements came awareness on the part of human beings of a superior nonhuman power by which people were created and upon which they depend. Having no viable prototype except themselves by which to formulate images in their own minds regarding the nature of this power, human beings eventually synthesized an anthropomorphic super-superman.

One says "eventually" in recognition of the wild hodgepodge of objects and images that at one time or another have received human adoration as possessing or symbolizing supranatural or at least suprahuman powers: sticks, stones, animals, trees, rivers, oceans, meterological phenomena, and all the rest. Even today, and under the umbrella of nominally monotheistic religions, there are (as we have seen) a bewildering multitude of lesser spirits: angels, devils, saints, and so forth, each having, so it is believed, supranatural influence on some people's lives.

A systematic detailed review of these images analyzing their perceptions as to the nature of the Supreme Being would provide valuable insight into the evolution of human thought, conditioned in part by advancing levels of cultural sophistication, in part by the varying circumstances under which people live, and possibly in part by actual changes (one would like to say improvements) in the genetic capabilities of the human brain itself. Some of this process of change can be traced in the Biblical-Quranic literature.

Chronologically the earliest image of God reported in the Bible was as Creator, a being who walked on earth in the form of man and talked to Adam and Eve. This was the image of God at the time when the Adam and Eve story and the accounts of the mythical patriarchs took shape. Noah was most prominent, and his story may be used to mark the close of an era so to speak. In this era He (God) was responsible for *all* humankind, but of course there were not too many people in those times. He punished and rewarded as suited His purpose.

Later, a somewhat similar entity appears as the God of Abraham, a being who occasionally appears in human form but more often through dreams or as a voice without body. However, for Abraham He is a personal proprietary God. Other individuals even in the same family have other gods, usually represented by small statuettes: graven images, many examples of which have been recovered in archeological digs.[1] In worshipping a single God, Abraham had broken away from the polytheism of his own family and of the semitic peoples who populated the fertile crescent area. There is always the question of course how much of the information we have about Abraham (and Isaac and Jacob and Joseph) is contemporaneous—how much represents later embellishments or even pious invention. Be it said that most has a truly authentic ring about it, but some as we shall point out must be questioned.

There is an unexplained gap between the "universal" God-for-all-men of the undatable creation myths, Adam and Eve, the tower of Babel and Noah's Flood, on the one hand, and the proprietary God of Abraham (ca. 1800 B.C.) and his descendants, on the other. Abraham's God was, however, a reasonable sort of person and could be bargained with.[2] The Covenant itself—central to Judaism and prominent also in Christianity and Islam—was a sort of bargain between God and Abraham.

At the time of Moses, a quite different God appears. He is withdrawn, terrifying, jealous, and vindictive. His presence is marked by fire, dense smoke, and the sound of a trumpet growing ever louder (Exodus 19:20). Sigmund Freud identifies Moses as an Egyptian rather than a Jew[3] and his God as a volcano god borrowed from the Midianites[4] among whom Moses had spent quite a few years as a fugitive from punishment in Egypt (for his part in the death of one of the Egyptian taskmasters whom he had seen abusing one of the Jewish workers). During that period of enforced exile with its opportunities to meditate on religious matters, Moses had married the daughter of a Midianite priest and thus would have become familiar with Midianite religious practices and beliefs. His earlier experiences in the household of Pharaoh's daughter would have imbued him with the sense of awe and mystery inspired by Egyptian religious rites.

The idea that Moses did in fact present a new perception of the supreme deity is scarcely debatable. We have suggested above that the withdrawn awesome characteristics of the deity of Moses's perception would have been drawn from the religious formulations of the Egyptians enhanced by their vast and magnificent temple compounds (he presumably knew the great temples at Karnak and Lux-

or). At the same time, God's appearances in the Exodus story unquestionably have volcanic attributes. Midian at that time (we are told by O. Eissfeldt, writing in The Cambridge Ancient History Vol. II, Ch. XXVI, (a) *The Exodus and Wanderings*) was a land with active volcanoes now dead.

Even the name of God had been changed; it was now not to be spoken by the common people and was known to priests only by the apparently meaningless initials JHWH, later popularized as Jahweh or Jehovah. The scribe who wrote down these matters, at least two or three centuries after Moses's time, thought it necessary to explain that, although the name had been changed, it was indeed the God of Abraham, Isaac, and Jacob (Exodus 3:13–15).

What had happened among the children of Israel during their long sojourn in Egypt, in the land of Goshen?[5] The personal God of Abraham had now changed in character (much of the change having been brought about as we believe by Moses himself). He had become a corporate God for the entire nation of the Israelites. He was not to be approached by the people as individuals, but only by a few chosen representatives (whether chosen by God or by the people was never quite clear). Moses was the first such chosen representative—and there was never another like him (Deuteronomy 34:10). He was followed by judges and then by kings, none of whom—not even the strongest—was on intimate speaking terms with God, nor deputized to exercise the power of God to anywhere near the same extent as Moses had.

It is purely a matter of speculation how much change in the religious beliefs and social mores of the children of Israel had been brought about by Egyptian influences during their sojourn there, and how much intermarriage there had been with Egyptians. However much it may have been, Judaism must be attributed largely to the single dominant personality of Moses, bent as it seems on erasing all memory of Egypt with its flesh pots and other abominations from the minds and souls of the children of Israel by means of their ordeal in the wilderness.[6]

Did Judaism as a distinctive religion originate entirely with Moses? In the latter case, the claim of Islam to be the older religion would take on new meaning; Islam claims to be based on the simple faith of Abraham exemplified in his personal submission to the will of God, while Moses had introduced a new perception of God, including the idea that there must be an intermediary between God and the people.

God's image as an exclusive possession of the Jewish people seems to have relaxed somewhat during the times of the later prophets. This change may be noted in the writings ascribed to Isaiah (flourished ca. 740–700 B.C.), seen in passages, some of which, though included in the Book of Isaiah, probably were written later, in the post-Babylonian-exile period (i.e., ca. 500 B.C.). By this time, the God of Israel had become more accessible. Strangers (i.e., non-Israelites) were to be allowed to present their petitions for His consideration with hope that He would listen. The following excerpts are from Isaiah:

> In days to come
> the mountain of the Lord's house
> shall be set over all other mountains,
>   lifted high above the hills.
> All the nations shall come streaming to it,
> And many peoples shall come and say,
> "Come, let us climb up on to the mountain of the Lord,
>   to the house of the God of Jacob
>   that he may teach us his ways
>   and we may walk in his paths."
> For instruction issues from Zion,
>   and out of Jerusalem comes the word of the Lord;
>   he will be judge between nations,
> arbiter among many peoples.
> They shall beat their swords into mattocks
>   and their spears into pruning knives;
> nation shall not lift sword against nation
>   nor ever again be trained for war.
>
>   (Isaiah 2:2–4)

> . . . The foreigner who has given his allegiance to the LORD
>   must not say
> "The LORD will keep me separate from his people forever." . . .
>   I will give them an everlasting name,
>   a name imperishable for all time.
> So too with the foreigners who give their allegiance to me, the
>   LORD
>   to minister to me and love my name

> and to become my servants,
> all who keep the sabbath undefiled
> and hold fast to my covenant:
> them will I bring to my holy hill
> and give them joy in my house of prayer.
> Their offerings and sacrifices shall be acceptable on my altar;
> for my house shall be called
> a house of prayer for all nations.

(Isaiah 56:1–8)

Another late change in the face of the anthropomorphic God, possibly reflecting a Babylonian influence, was the introduction of the idea of Satan, whereby the character of God was freed from accountability for man's sins and errors. This created a more idealistic but also a more puzzling image. God now was all-good and all-beneficent, yet despite being all-powerful, he somehow (and for reasons never very satisfactorily explained) allowed this fallen angel—his insubordinate subordinate—free reign to go about thwarting his purposes.

Later still, Jesus of Nazareth presented, in a much more fully developed form, this perception of a *universal* God, which had been tentatively advanced by Isaiah and is found also in the writings of other later prophets. John the Baptist and Jesus both inveigh against the racial "apartheid" of the Pharisees of their day: "vipers' brood" (we might now say "WASPs"!). Descent from Abraham meant nothing per se; a humble, trusting, loving heart everything.

The God of Christ's perception is a heavenly Father—Father to *all* who receive his word by the Holy Spirit (Logos), no longer proprietary to the children of Israel as a hereditary right—though they *are* the ones who first recognized Him and preserved His worship. Even Jesus's own disciples, steeped as they were in Jewish tradition, were slow to catch the full implications of this point. It was, of course, anathema to the Scribes, Pharisees, doctors of law, and all who made up the fundamentalist establishment of Judaism at that time. It may still be anathema to orthodox extremists in modern Judaism.[7]

However, one should take note that even Jesus himself, on one occasion at least, betrayed the same spirit of Jewish apartheid. While visiting in the region of Tyre, he turned away the pleas of a Canaanite woman on behalf of her daughter, saying to her: "I was sent to the lost sheep of the house of Israel, and to them alone." Nevertheless the woman persisted, and he finally said: "Woman, what faith you have! Be it as you wish!" And from that moment her daughter was restored to health (Matthew 15:21–28; similarly in Mark 7:24–30). For the Christian Church the logjam was finally broken by the Apostle Peter's famous dream in which the Lord said to Peter: "It is not for you to call profane what God counts clean" (Acts 10:9–16).

The heavenly Father as portrayed by Jesus through parables and by admonition was (as noted in the preceding chapter) loving, caring, forgiving, and patient. He provided for and welcomed all humankind on the basis of an accepting inner spirit. He had a relationship with His worshippers similar to that of a wise and kindly human father to his very small children—children trusting completely in their father's wisdom and in his ability to provide whatever they would need. Indeed all of Jesus's ministry seems attuned to that child-like mentality, living for the here and now and giving no thought for the morrow. "Except you become as one of these (trusting children) you will not enter the kingdom of heaven."

After Jesus's death, even during the lifetimes of his remaining disciples, this image of God was lost or greatly modified. In its place appeared an image of God as ruler and law giver. As Caesar on Earth, so God in heaven! He was represented on Earth by His premier vicar, the Bishop of Rome (later the Pope) and by an extensive regional hierarchy not unlike that of the contemporary Roman Empire. By the time of St. Augustine (354–430), this had been turned around: because it was that way in heaven, it should be so on Earth! Needless to say, this was not the *only* image of God, but it came to be the prevailing orthodox image; others became heretical.

Also, the orthodox image became more and more complex as the concept of a triune God evolved with all its ramifications. Christ then became a coequal part in the theological concept of Trinity, of the same substance as God (necessarily therefore a disembodied spirit rather than, as he himself claimed to be, the Son of Man and, of course, also the Son of God in the sense that all true believers have a father-son relationship to the heavenly Father). When William Blake depicted Christ as the Lamb, it was apparently as a paragon among human beings motivated and guided by the Holy Spirit/Logos—not this theologically disembodied segment of the Trinity.

The Trinity particularly bothered Muhammad, whose simple credo is built around the affirmation that there is no god but God. One of his revelations, recorded in the Quran, is of a conversation between God and Jesus son of Mary (note: *not* son of God though he echoes the Gospel story of Mary chaste and pure impregnated by the Holy Spirit), in which God asks Jesus whether he had told men that he was God. Jesus answers that he told them only what He (God) had told him to say. [This obviously did not include any statement remotely suggesting that Christ himself was God, nor that God in person—or through His Holy Spirit as proxy—had been his father in the biological sense (Sura 5:110—116). This passage is, incidentally, one place in the Quran where the phrase Holy Spirit—*ruh al-qudus*—is used in the sense of power to perform miracles.]

The God of Muhammad's perception, Allah, embodied a confusing mixture of rejection in principle but acknowledgement in reality of an anthropomorphic spiritual entity. On the one hand, Allah did not sleep, or sit, or stand, or walk. He did not beget nor was he begotten. To suggest any of these things was a most heinous of sins. At the same time Allah made himself manifest to human beings in a great many very human ways. He did select Muhammad as his messenger and did deliver His messages in a particular human language (actually, a strikingly vigorous, new human art form, Arabic rhymed prose). This by definition had to be a human medium in order to be within human comprehension. He did send down a great many revelations of divine law, which happened to fit the pressing judicial-legislative needs of a primitive semi-pastoral-nomadic, semi-mercantile society such as that over which Muhammad was presiding. With what some now regard as delightful irony, Aisha, Muhammad's favorite wife, is reputed to have said to him on one occasion that it was a very remarkable thing how Allah always came to his rescue when he had gotten himself into a tight corner.[8]

A twentieth century perception regarding the nature of God was delineated by the psychoanalyst and author Erich Fromm (1900–1980), lecturing at the New School for Social Research some years ago. Fromm reported that his patients generally thought of God as an all-powerful corporate executive. He was chairman and chief executive officer of Universe, Inc., a multinational corporation. People were His employees. They often had suggestions as to ways in which their own job could be made pleasanter, their particular department could be run more efficiently, and/or employee morale improved. Prayer was a sort of employee suggestion system. They accepted the fact that the C.E.O. could not act on all the suggestions. Presumably He heard them all and weighed their merit as to whether they would conflict with operations in other departments or raise other problems. That was fair enough. Nevertheless, they generally had the feeling that God was a person: kindly, fair-minded, a reasonable sort of C.E.O., and if a matter was important enough, and they could get His ear, He would fix things up.

Fromm, of course, was gently poking fun at that image. He suggested that there could be only two valid ways to relate to the Supreme Being: (1) in a spirit of joy and gratitude for being part of His world; or (2) in a spirit of remorse and contrition for real or imagined sin, seeking atonement. Atonement, Fromm defined, as the feeling of "at-one-ment" after estrangement—comparable to getting back on the payroll of the company (Universe, Inc., or one of its subsidiaries) after having been suspended or fired for cause.

People naturally assume that the God mentioned at the opening of Genesis and throughout the Bible is, as the Reverend Isaac Watts put it, "through endless years the same." Given a half-dozen or more different names in Hebrew and Aramaic, with their translations into Greek, Latin, and many other languages—and 99 names in Arabic—He is nevertheless, or so most modern readers assume, basically one and the same entity throughout. But not so! While awareness of a supra-human power who created human beings, and upon whom they depend for existence, is so widespread as to constitute virtual scientific proof that there is, for all humankind, an entity that people call God, human perceptions of that entity are quite diverse. The entity is as real as human existence is real; the perceptions are ephemeral. We have called this reality Deus Sapiens to link this concept with the mind of man, without anthropomorphic implications.

People's extremely diverse perceptions as to the nature of that supreme being cancel each other out and render the idea of one single anthropomorphic God "through endless years the same" rather ridiculous. Human perceptions of an anthropomorphic God are more accurately described as mirror images of the needs and aspirations, the moral value systems, and the cultural preprogramming of the individual at any particular time. All things change and with them, people's images of God change. One must search elsewhere for something that is truly "through endless years the same." As stated repeatedly herein, that something is Deus Universalis.

NOTES

1. The statement that different people even in the same family might have different gods is strikingly illustrated in the biblical story of Jacob's confrontation with his father-in-law Laban (Genesis 31:19–35). Laban was a *very* close relative indeed. He was the son of Abraham and Sarah's brother (Abraham and his wife Sarah were both children of the same father by different mothers). He was therefore double first cousin as well as brother-in-law to Abraham and Sarah's only son Isaac, who had married Laban's sister Rebecca. Their child, Jacob, had been sent off by Rebecca to Laban (that is to say, to her brother, who was Jacob's uncle) to avoid the anger and vengeance of Esau arising out of the trickery whereby Jacob had gotten his blind and somewhat dotty old father Isaac to give him the inheritance intended for his older twin brother, Esau. During his sojourn in Laban's camp, Jacob had shown himself much more skillful in animal husbandry than Laban's own sons and had married both of his daughters, Leah and Rachel. He himself had been tricked into marrying Leah. He loved only Rachel. He was fleeing now, back to take up his own inheritance, taking from Laban what he could take. His motive was partly to avoid the jealousy of Laban's sons and partly fear that Laban would not live up to the terms they had agreed upon. The passage reads:

> When Laban the Aramean had gone to shear his sheep, Rachel stole her father's household gods, and Jacob deceived Laban, keeping his departure secret. . . . When Laban overtook him . . . Laban said to Jacob, "What have you done? You have deceived me and carried off my daughters as though they were captives taken in war. . . . It is in my power to do you an injury, but yesterday the God of your father spoke to me . . . but why did you steal my gods?"
>
> Jacob answered, "I was afraid; I thought you would take your daughters from me by force. Whoever is found in possession of your gods shall die for it. . . ."

Jacob did not know that Rachel had stolen the gods. Laban searched everywhere without finding anything and finally came to Rachel's tent:

Now she had taken the household gods and put them in the camel-bag and was sitting on them. Laban went through everything and found nothing. Rachel said to her father, "Do not take it amiss, sir, that I cannot rise in your presence: the common lot of woman is upon me." So for all his search Laban did not find his household gods.

(New English translation)

This story sheds considerable light on the primitive theology of that period. Abraham had broken with family tradition in selecting a single God. The idea that God could not and must not be represented by graven images may have been inherent in Abraham's perception, or may have been added in the time of Moses, five or six centuries later. Usually, each head-of-household had his own personal God or gods, and his prosperity and well-being was related to their power as much or more than to the owner's own acumen and effort. What Rachel had expected to gain by depriving her father of his household gods is obscure. Perhaps she too thought they conferred power or at least good luck.

W. F. Albright, the distinguished biblical archeologist, points out a striking anachronism in this story: camel-bags would not have been found in Jacob's luggage, as the camel had not yet been domesticated. The first authentic biblical references to the use of camels date from the time of King David, five or six centuries later. In Jacob's time, pack animals used by caravans would probably have been donkeys or mules.

2. Illustrated by the delightful story of Abraham's hospitality to God and his angels, who were on their way to punish Sodom and Gomorrah for their wickedness, this story (Genesis 18:1–23) first describes Abraham's bedouin hospitality, then describes his delightful haggle with God, trying to persuade him to spare those two cities, or at least some of the people in them. Abraham's nephew Lot lived there (hence his special interest). Scholars accept Abraham as a historical figure, though he lived long before earliest written records and left no archeological traces. One may assume from his obvious affluence, acquired during an earlier journey to Egypt and sustained throughout his life, that he was a world-class bargainer.

The inquiring historian must question sharply whether the reported negotiation with the Lord actually occurred. Nevertheless, to unnumbered millions of the faithful it is very real. It provides what appears to be an authentic portrayal of manners typical of the times, and of God as a reasonable sort of person, a person from whom one could occasionally gain concessions through argument—just like the better sort of people with whom the author of this charming story met every day in the normal course of events.

The story seems based on plausible facts. There are ruins near the southern end of the Dead Sea that archeologists identify as Sodom and Gomorrah. That indeed was the area chosen by Lot when he and his Uncle Abraham parted ways (Genesis 13:5–13). No geological evidence supports the thesis of any volcanic action which would have rained fire and brimstone in that particular area nor upon those cities, at least not for many thousands of years before Abraham's time. However, the ancients were familiar with the destruction that can be meted out by volcanic action.

Some observers argue (quite convincingly) that the whole Sodom and Gomorrah story was pure invention, a sort of Uncle Remus story, included in the canon not because anybody thought it happened, but in order to strike terror into the hearts of the children of Israel and thereby deter them from engaging in sodomy and sinful practices of similar nature. If so, it is a masterpiece of Jewish moralizing, imagination, and skill in storytelling.

3. The brilliant and respected (but controversial) Austrian neurologist and founder of psychoanalysis, Sigmund Freud (1856–1939), added a novel twist to the speculations about this obscure period in Jewish history. In a series of three papers, published in book form in the year of his death (1939), *Moses and Monotheism*, Freud contends that—Moses was not Jewish at all but rather an Egyptian of royal parentage, brought up perhaps in a Jewish family. In Freud's scenario, that particular Moses (Moses being a very common component in Egyptian names, e.g., Atmose, Thutmose, and many other combinations) had been a loyal follower of the Pharaoh Amenophis IV (Akhenaten, 1379–1362 B.C.) and a devotee of his revolutionary monotheistic religion of sun worship (the sun being perceived as source of all life and energy).

When Akhenaten died and the priests restored the old state religion, this Egyptian Moses was determined to find a way to perpetuate monotheism. He did in fact "choose" (hence the myth of a chosen people) a heterogeneous group of disgruntled Semites who happened to be living in the province of Goshen. That area, being in the northeast corner of the Nile delta, was nearest to the land of Canaan. The people of that land (Canaan) had a religion that incorporated many features similar to the polytheistic state religion of Egypt; it would therefore be proper retaliation for this Egyptian Moses to take that land and destroy that religion.

In Freud's scenario, this Egyptian Moses did lead those people into the wilderness, where he was perhaps eventually murdered. That scenario at least would account for the Jewish people's ever-present national feelings of guilt. Somewhere, perhaps at Kadesh-Barnea, the contingent of Semites from Egypt was joined (still following Freud's scenario) by some of the Habiru, a group of nomadic tribesmen, known from the Amarna letters (written to the Pharaoh Akhenaten by his governors then stationed in Syria/Palestine). The Habiru are characterized in these letters as homeless marauders and very troublesome. Freud suggests that his Egyptian Moses had made a considerable start at least at formulating or adapting from sources along the way the traditions that were eventually consolidated into Judaism and preserved in the Torah. For example, Freud holds that Moses introduced circumcision previously unknown to the Semites. Freud identifies JHWH as a volcano god worshipped by the Midianites of northern Arabia (at that time a region of volcanoes). He equates "Adonai," another early name for God found in Hebrew scriptures, with "Aten," the sun, and so forth. Other later leaders, some of whom perhaps carried the name Moses and were therefore confused with the original Moses, continued this process of "creating" Jewish tradition.

Regardless of the historical merit of Freud's theories about this obscure period of Jewish history, his observations about the psychoanalytical aspects command attention. His observation about national guilt is of interest, and in particular his contention that the "stubborn and arrogant" assumption by the Jewish people that they are God's chosen people is largely to blame for their recurrent persecution and repression, a sort of lemming syndrome of proliferation and destruction.

This thesis takes on special poignancy in that it was developed during his last years in Austria and was written in London as a refugee from the impending Nazi holocaust. One pauses to consider this statement from different viewpoints. To be sure, the "chosen people" idea inevitably clashed with the Nazi's "master race" idea—and the Nazis had the guns! But how important was that as a cause of the German Jewish holocaust? Certainly many and, by some reports, more of the victims of Nazi death camps were people of other "inferior" races: Gypsies, Poles, Byelorussians, and so on—peoples who would not have waved the red flag of chosenness in front of the Nazi bull.

4. Moses's sojourn in the land of the Midianites (now the northwestern part of Saudi Arabia) is well established by the biblical record. Except for Freud's reference, little or nothing is known about alleged volcano worship among the Midianites of that era (presumed ca. 1250 B.C.). There *is* scholarly support for the idea that there were active volcanoes in that region at that time, although none have been active in recent years. There *is* strong argument that the Mount Sinai of the Ten Commandments/Golden Calf happenings was not the modern Mount Sinai of the Sinai peninsula, but rather a mountain in the Midianites' region. Moses's vision of the burning bush that was not consumed and the voice of God that he heard at that time, may be linked to some sort of natural phenomenon (some minor volcanic eruption perhaps or a seepage of natural gas that had somehow gotten ignited) or may, of course, be regarded simply as an illusory vision, a mirage created within a highly gifted, hypersensitive religious imagination preindoctrinated with a lore in which fire and volcanic action held a central role.

5. A brief review of what is known about the history of Egypt during this confused period may serve to place the Jewish sojourn there into some sort of perspective. It is assumed that Joseph, the great-grandson of Abraham, was sold into slavery in Egypt sometime in the mid-seventeenth century, say around 1650 B.C. or earlier. At that time, the weak XIII Dynasty (1786–1633 B.C.) was still in office, with a rapid succession of weak Pharaohs ruling through strong prime ministers. Also in office was the XIV Dynasty (ca. 1786–1603), the "seventy-six kings of Xoïs" ruling in the northwestern corner of the Nile delta, and therefore not a factor in our narrative. Also ruling contemporaneously were three other dynasties: XV (1674–1567), XVI (ca. 1684–1567), and XVII (ca. 1650–1567). The two former were Hyksos rulers, Semitic chieftains from the desert country of the northeast; the last were shadowy Egyptian kings ruling from Thebes. All three of these last-named dynasties were terminated in 1567 B.C. by Nebpehtyre Amosis, the first pharaoh of the XVIII Dynasty, whose personal rule extended 24 years from 1570 to 1546 B.C. His dynastic name was Amenhotep I. This dynasty and its successor, the XIX, brought Egyptian power and culture to the highest levels that it was destined to attain. The children of Israel were in residence during all this period.

For many years prior to Joseph, Semites had been common in Egypt, mostly as slaves captured in raiding expeditions or brought by slave traders, as in the case of Joseph. Others came as traders or managers of the caravans that carried goods to and from Syria and farther away. Beginning in the seventeenth century B.C., or perhaps somewhat earlier, Semitic chieftains and their followers came, apparently in the manner of condottieri, driven in part by famines in their home country, but attracted by the richness and weakness of the rulers at that time of Egypt. At first, the Egyptian pharaohs, unable to repel them, employed them as mercenaries and officers of state. About 1684 in one case and 1674 in another, two of these condottieri chieftains simply set up rule in their own names in territory that they had previously controlled (apparently) in the name of the Pharaoh.

Jacob and his entourage, 11 sons and their wives and families, the children of Israel, seem to have been a part of this movement. The circumstance that they came in peace and that a member of their household (Joseph) was already in a position of great power (exercising all the authority of the Pharaoh except his titular roles) led to their very favorable reception. The area over which Joseph's Pharaoh exercised effective control was, however, probably quite limited.

Joseph's story is difficult to fit into this complex picture. One's inclination is to connect his regime as prime minister with one or more of the later Pharaohs in the XIII Dynasty. There is nothing in the Egyptian records with which one can connect his regime or date it. If the biblical narrative is followed literally, it must have lasted at least 14 years (seven years of crop surpluses and seven of famine)—and must have been sociologically and economically among the most noteworthy in all Egyptian history. Joseph did not distribute the accumulated surplus gratis but sold it for cash. When the people's cash ran out he took in the name of the Pharaoh, their cattle and land (except the land of the priests, many of whom were in any case·already pensioners of the crown). One must note that Joseph had been given as wife the daughter of one of the priests attached to the great religious center at On (near Cairo), an event that may or may not have influenced his decision in this regard. One would like to think not.

The effect of this policy (if correctly reported in the Bible) would have been to convert Egypt from a nation of small independent landowners to a nation where all the land and livestock was owned by the crown but assigned back its previous owners on a sharecropping or tenant farmer basis.

Through Joseph's influence and the favor of the reigning Pharaoh, the children of Israel were assigned some of the best lands in Egypt. (One wonders what provision was made for the previous owners whom they displaced.) This land apparently was in the northeast corner of the Nile delta (the land of Goshen) and was adjacent to grazing land outside the delta, where there would be suitable pasturage for the herds and flocks that they had brought with them, because "all shepherds are an abomination to the Egyptians" (Genesis 46:34). They hated grazing livestock, as one would expect in a nation predominately dependent on crops. Four centuries later their descendants were still living in the same area.

The biblical report makes it clear that their numbers had increased exponentially over those four centuries, to the point of becoming a matter of alarm to the Egyptian governors—though the numbers given in the Exodus account must not be taken at face value. This "population explosion" bespeaks tolerable living conditions and successful adaptation to the settled agricultural life of Egypt, but curiously tells us nothing about any Israelite participation in the cultural and religious life of Egypt during the great flowering of that period. It also bespeaks a strong tribal cohesion, always characteristic of Semitic peoples, and perhaps one of the factors in the Egyptian governors' alarm.

It may be inferred, in the absence of any supporting documentation, that the long and glorious reign of Rameses II (1304–1237 B.C.) represented the nemesis of the Jewish occupation—"the Pharaoh who knew not Joseph." Moses's plagues and pestilences may be related to the misfortunes that befell Egypt in the last years of Rameses's reign and under his successor Merneptah (1236–1223). The so-called Israel Stela is dated in this latter period. It includes the phrase: "Israel is waste and has no seed." According to the writer of Chapter XXIII in *The Cambridge Ancient History* (vol. II, part 2, p.

234), this is taken to mean that the Jews were already in Palestine. It seems rather to mean that they had all left Egypt and were still in the wilderness—had not yet shown up in the land of Canaan. If they had, the Egyptians would know of it. This is apparently the only direct reference to Israel in any Egyptian text.

It may be that Rameses's far-reaching building ambitions created a need for impressed labor, which probably fell with equal misery on all elements in the Egyptian population, but the Israelites were more recalcitrant and audible in their groaning, and more able to articulate and preserve the memories of their oppression, so that their experiences could be written down by the earliest scribes some three centuries later.

However that may be, the Book of Exodus opens with Israelite labor gangs working on Rameses II's projects at the cities of Pithom and Rameses, both well-known archeological sites in the northeast delta area (Exodus 1:12).

We must leave this review of the Israelites' sojourn in Egypt almost exactly where we began it—with no solid information at all regarding their cultural and religious adaptation to the very rich and vigorous happenings in Egypt during this period.

One may surmise that some of the stories that have come down from the patriarchal age and earlier were handed down all during this period by word of mouth and have reached us more or less intact; others must have been invented later and draped over the shoulders of the legendary patriarchs. Any stories that may have originated among the Israelites arising out of their Egyptian experiences seem to have been lost during the Exodus sojourn in the wilderness or expunged later from the record. As suggested above, this may well have been exactly what Moses wanted to have happen.

Information for this brief and sketchy overview of the confusing history of Egypt during the Israelites' sojourn in that country is derived largely from *The Cambridge Ancient History*, vol. II, parts 1 and 2; *The New Columbia Encyclopedia*; and John Van Seters' *The Hyksos, A New Investigation* (1966). There have been many newer theories advanced as to the dates of Joseph's regime, the dates of the Exodus, the duration of the sojourn in the wilderness, the numbers of people who had departed with Moses, whether they were in fact all the Israelites or purely Israelites and, if not, what admixture of other dissatisfied elements, and so forth and so on.

6. A particularly interesting and challenging study of the wilderness experience as it is presented in the Torah has been prepared by Richard Adamiak and published with a foreword by Noel Freedman under the title *Justice and History in the Old Testament/The Evolution of Divine Retribution in the Historiographies of the Wilderness Generation* (1982). The work of a half-dozen different scribes is here traced, each with a certain slant attributable in part

perhaps to the personality of the writer and in part to the conditions of the audiences for whom he was writing. The careful reader will be discouraged and confused by irreconcilable differences in the presumably factual material presented by different writers, but will be reconciled by the thought that this is not so much a recital of facts as a panorama of the development of Jewish religious thought.

The identity of the different writers may be reviewed in various biblical and general encyclopedia articles relating to these matters. Doubtless different scholars would present different opinions. Very tentatively, the following checklist is offered to provide broad perspectives on the writing of this and other material included in the Torah:

J   a writer probably working at the time of Israel's greatest glory, under Kings David and Solomon.

E   a writer probably 100 years later, working at a time of deteriorating political fortunes.

JE   a later editor who combined in his writing material largely derived from the two previous writers in a way that cannot be unscrambled and that has its own slant. He wrote perhaps two centuries after J and one century after E.

D   the Deuteronomic writer; late but preexilic.

Dtr   the Deuteronomistic writer. Probably written during the Exile (Babylonian Captivity).

P   the priestly writer. Probably written during the Exile (Babylonian Captivity).

7. Laymen and outsiders today sometimes see Jewishness as a form of apartheid, an exclusive elitist club from which the members emerge only to acquire the necessities and in many cases a generous helping of the luxuries of this world. In many cases, they also make great contributions to the general well-being—but always return and shut the doors. For a Jew (according to this scenario) to accept fully and/or be fully accepted by the outside world would be to lose Jewishness: to become as one with the ten lost tribes! Ardently as one (if a Jew) may desire to be loved as a human being, admired, accepted, and regarded as morally right, it is necessary to be at least somewhat hated and despised in order to maintain one's sense of "belonging" within that exclusive club—and necessary (collectively) to maintain the club as a viable entity.

This state of affairs has persisted for at least 2,000 years. The religious society of Pharisees was built on the puritanism of earlier reforms by Ezra and Nehemiah. It was founded in the times of the Maccabees to isolate and insulate the Jewish people from the Hellenizing influences to which they were then exposed. A century later, John the Baptist and Jesus of Nazareth waged, as noted above, an unsuccessful battle against what Freud calls this "stubborn arrogance." Nineteen centuries later, Sigmund Freud had taken up, as noted in note 3, the same issue.

Jesus had attempted to substitute the kingdom of heaven as the sheltering "club," the messianic state promised to the Jewish people. It is not clear what Sigmund Freud would substitute. Most people would agree that some sort of "club," some special place or belief where one can feel that one really "belongs," is altogether desirable for the mental and spiritual well-being of humankind. Many, however, would agree also that it cannot be arranged in just one group's interest. Any sort of club must be tolerable or at least viable in relation to other people's interest and their competing "clubs."

8. Muhammad (flourished A.D. 610–632) had grown up in Mecca in an environment where primitive polytheistic (one might almost say shamanistic) religious practices shared the stage with the teachings and practices of both Jews and Christians. The former were represented by small colonies of Jews, some no doubt from the diaspora, settled in oases where they could make a living growing dates and other produce. The latter were represented by a few individuals, probably heretics seeking respite from the persecutions of the Byzantine church. Muhammad as a child also may have been exposed to the stories of caravan traders travelling to and fro, carrying spices and other precious luxury goods from Yemen, India, and beyond, to Syria and the port cities of the eastern Mediterranean for shipment to Rome, Greece, Gaul, and other prosperous markets. Indeed he himself later made at least two trips by caravan and stayed on the way at monasteries and talked to the monks.

One has the impression of Muhammad at this age as a quiet, withdrawn, very intelligent, intensely attentive boy, absorbing deeply a variety of impressions regarding Judaism and Christianity (both in its Byzantine orthodox formulation and in the formulations of the several Eastern heresies: Nestorian, Arian, Jacobite, or whatever). When at the age of about 40 his religious nature became the dominant factor in his life, he first sought recognition as a Jewish prophet. He may have had somewhere in his subconscious memory the prayer attributed to Solomon at the dedication of his temple (ca. 950 B.C., but probably written much later), opening Jewish religious tradition to all peoples and sharing their God's justice and mercy with others beside lineal descendants of Israel:

> The foreigner too, the man who does not belong to thy people Israel, but has come from a distant land because of thy great fame and thy strong hand and arm outstretched, when he comes and prays towards this house, hear from heaven thy dwelling and respond to the call which the foreigner makes to thee, so that like thy people Israel all

peoples of the earth may know thy fame and fear thee, and learn that this house which I built bears thy name.

> (2 Chronicles 6:32–33 Nearly identical in 1 Kings 8:41–43.)

Muhammad apparently accepted Jewish specialness but he and his companions were not exactly strangers or foreigners. They were descended from Ishmael, Abraham's oldest son. Muhammad may have focused his attention on the passage quoted above, allegedly spoken by Solomon at the dedication of his great temple in Jerusalem (ca. 950 B.C.) but, as we have noted, coming to us in texts known to have been written four or five centuries later and reflecting, no doubt, a later stage in the evolution of Jewish religious philosophy than would have prevailed in Solomon's day.

There is no corroborating record of Muhammad's request to be accepted officially as a Jewish prophet. Evidently, if submitted, the request was rejected or ignored. Meanwhile, Muhammad first taught his followers to pray facing Jerusalem, just as Solomon had said. When Jewish rejection had become apparent, he changed the qibla toward Mecca, long recognized among Bedouin Arabs as a holy place and center for their primitive religious rites.

As revelation after revelation came to Muhammad, originating as we believe in the vast subconscious storehouse of impressions gathered in his early years, Allah emerged as a purified (purified in Muhammad's mind) version of the God of Abraham, which Judaism and Christianity had (in his view) corrupted with erroneous doctrine and "unbelief" (a word with special theological meaning in Islam). Muhammad confirmed all that God/JHWH/ the Lord/ Allah had said to the prophets of Israel and to Christ, but rejected the interpretations and theological formulations that their followers had made of those messages. The Quran and Torah have much in common.

As a sort of footnote to the above, we should make note of a very recent and as yet untested theory put forward by Kamal Salibi, a highly respected professor of history at the American University of Beirut. Salibi has noted a remarkable series of coincidences between place names in the Asir (a region in Arabia extending along the Red Sea and inland south of Mecca) and those associated with early Jewish history hitherto universally held to have been located in Palestine. What implications this may have for the unraveling of biblical history of the patriarchal period remains to be seen. Wherever they originally came from prior to the sojourn in the land of Goshen, there can be little question that the Jews did go to Palestine.

10   Revelation Rationally Considered

Revelation is a variety of religious experience, necessarily involving the composition, arrangement, and activity of neurons stimulated and responding in special ways. Revelation, regardless of what stimuli evoke or induce it, is essentially a *human* phenomenon, shaped and colored by genetic and environmental factors peculiar to the individual who undergoes the experience. Revelation—hitherto promulgated as the Word of God, and therefore sacrosanct eternal truth—is identified now rather as the product of the Holy Spirit/Logos (the Inner Voice, to use Quaker terminology), a form of intuitive inspiration originating within the psyche or soul of some specially gifted human being. It demands and deserves to be treated with profound respect, but may nevertheless be weighed and evaluated dispassionately on a scale that measures wisely and impartially its beneficial (or possibly harmful) effects for humankind.

Revelation may be vouchsafed to a genius or a person of less gifted intellect, even to persons whose mentality is temporarily or permanently deranged. Some revelations reflect great insight into human nature and may approach the stature of "eternal truth" (eternal as long as man exists). Some are quite petty or at least of very limited application. A few are purely self-serving and, from the point of view of those whose interests are negatively served, pure humbug.

Seen in this light, the Mosaic "revelations" range in importance from those that establish the spiritual identity of Israel and set forth its basic moral code to important issues relating to public health and on to lesser matters of ritual and behavior. Finally they come down to finicky mundane matters such as spelling out in surprisingly meticulous detail the God-decreed(?) measurements and materials to be used in the manufacture of the tabernacle and ark, and still farther down the scale to self-serving propaganda. Not all of these revelations should be regarded as uniformly sacrosanct: none of them is an immutable eternal truth pronounced by a non-molecular but otherwise anthropomorphic supreme being "up there."

The hypothesis set forth in previous chapters holds that these revelations took shape unconsciously deep within the mysterious repository of knowledge, motivation, orientation, etc. (tentatively called psyche) possessed by some religiously gifted individual who by some mysterious mental process projected them out and received them back (our simplistic radar analogy), and thereupon became consciously aware of them, deeming them to be the voice of God. Regardless of the merit of this hypothesis as to their origin, there is no question but that they were received and processed in strictly human minds. They were communicated to others and in the process of communication were subjected to further processing by a succession of human minds down to the present.

Among the many towering personalities who possessed minds capable of participating *and* who were positioned to participate in this process, Moses stands out above all the rest. Clearly Abraham six centuries before him also had such a mind. Others whose names we do not know—scholars, scribes, priests before and after Moses (but mostly after)—also had such minds, but lacked the charisma or historic occasion to make a name for themselves. It is the task of the inquiring historian to try to determine to what extent the revelations attributed for example to Abraham or to Moses are both authentic *and* accurately transmitted, to what extent authentic material has been embellished in the process of transmission, and to what extent pious invention has been grafted onto the root-stock of these two great prophets for the purpose of gaining credence and acceptance. Pious inventors may be persons of high motivation who have had the welfare and aggrandizement of Israel at heart just as sincerely and devoutly as the primary actors.

All three elements are present in the material assembled, edited, and promulgated by the priest/prophet Ezra in 444 B.C. as the Torah or Pentateuch. Material that is authentically old, the embellishments and the inventions all equally had the purpose and effect of shaping Judaism as a religion, and shaping Jewish outlook or "character" into a cohesive people or nation. The timetable of these revelations and the events with which they are associated is as follows:

19th century B.C.   Abraham (monotheism, covenant)

13th century B.C.   Moses (Exodus, foundation of Judaism)

10th century B.C.   David and Solomon (creation of Hebrew literature, the temple, first written history, Israel's proudest days)

6th century B.C.   Babylonian Captivity (new dimensions added to Judaism)

5th century B.C.   Ezra (definitive recession of Torah)

As outlined below, it is our contention that Moses and his collaborators created much new "history," and probably obliterated much old history regarding the Jewish people. To do so was a necessary part of his drive to create a cohesive, aggressive, and effective nation. In speaking here of "history" created, we refer particularly to reports about what the Lord said to Abraham and the patriarchs, upon which Judaism is founded, especially the Covenant.

Central to the formation of Judaism is Abraham's famous Covenant with the Lord, a form of "revelation." This is mentioned perhaps a dozen times in the Torah, each time differing from the others in some detail. It is also mentioned several times in the Quran. The versions which come down to us make it clear that Ishmael (Abraham's son by the slave-girl Haggar) was excluded from the Covenant (Genesis 17:19–20). Thus this Covenant applied only to his descendants through his half-sister, who was also his wife, Sarah. One such descendant, Esau, was however tricked out of his inheritance by Jacob. The story is set forth in Genesis, Chapter 27 (complete). The very fact that the event is set forth at such great length and is so specific in its details suggests later embellishment. Some may take it as an indication that the children of Jacob (Israel)—probably many generations later—felt the need to invent a plausible story to establish as "undisputable fact" that they only were intended, and that Esau, later the nation of Edom with whom Israel was often at war, was specifically excluded from the Covenant. The specific exclusion of Ishmael, traditional ancestor of the Arabs, is not mentioned in the

Quranic references, but on the other hand there is no desire to be included. Abraham was the founder of *Islam*. The Jewish people received that inheritance but later became "unbelievers" (a word which Muhammad uses with special venom).

The most complete single statement of the Covenant is at Genesis 17:1–22. It contains three separate elements. These we take to have been made part of Jewish national tradition at different times, and for different purposes, brought together by later scribes who told and retold the story for different audiences at different times.

The first element was the requirement that Abraham himself and all males in his entourage (probably at that time several hundred persons) and all his male descendants forever, undergo the ritual surgery, circumcision.

The second element was Abraham's undertaking for himself and his descendents down to the remotest generations to have no other gods but God, with God undertaking to keep Abraham and his descendents forever in His special care. This exclusive relationship was circumscribed, as noted above, so that it applied only to the children of Israel.

As the third element of the Covenant, the Lord gave to Abraham and his descendents forever (again, effectively limited to the children of Israel) the land of Canaan to occupy and to rule. We have not been able to find this element mentioned in the Quran. The boundaries of the land of Canaan are given quite differently in different versions of the Covenant, an observation that suggests the effect of different scribes writing at different times during the rise and fall of Jewish national geo-political fortunes.

The first element, the ritual of circumcision, has always seemed a curious thing to have been given such a leading position in the development of Judaism. However, the biblical story does say that the Lord rewarded Abraham through the birth of a son to Sarah just a year after the event. Up to that time she had been barren and had given up hope of having children.[1] The historical importance of this "revelation" becomes more apparent if one comes to the conclusion that without circumcision Isaac would not have been born, and that Abraham's patrimony would have passed to Ishmael, his son by Sarah's Egyptian maidservant Haggar. It would of course be pure speculation whether, in that case, there would have been any Covenant, and what the provisions might have been.

The *Hastings Dictionary of the Bible* provides a scholarly discussion as to the origin of the practice of circumcision and concludes that it seems to have had its origin in very ancient times among peoples residing in Africa. Sigmund Freud, in developing his extensively researched thesis that Moses was an Egyptian, is quite clear that circumcision had been practiced by the Egyptians long before it became a custom among Semitic peoples. Historians by and large do not agree with the thesis that Moses was Egyptian but cannot fail to respect the serious effort Freud had made to assemble all relevant historical data. It may therefore be suggested that the ritual was indeed ancient Egyptian in origin and Abraham became aware of it during his momentous journey into Egypt some years previous to the revelation that established the Covenant, or at least this part of it. In any case, this part of the Covenant seems authentically pre-Mosaic.

The revelations that Abraham should apply circumcision to himself and to all males of his entourage would have come (as we believe all revelations come) as a form of religious experience, a mysterious amalgam—need we say it again—arising out of the subconscious resources of that sector of the human mind, which we call psyche or soul. That it should have come just at that critical moment in Abraham and Sarah's personal lives (she at the end of her childbearing years) is one of those unexplainable phenomena that one associates with the incidence of very great genius among human beings. In any case, it was not a passing whim. Abraham took this revelation (in whatever form it came to him) to be the will of the Lord, and he obeyed. Since the relationship with the Lord was with him alone, and he was absolute ruler over everyone in his entourage, there was no need to hold a meeting nor to ask or persuade anyone; he simply ordered it done to all males, and it was done.

The antiquity of this part of the Covenant is further attested by a rather horrible story that takes up the entire thirty-fourth chapter of Genesis. Dinah, the daughter whom Leah had borne to Jacob, had been taken, against her will apparently, by Schechem, the son of the ruler of a city near which Jacob had pitched his tents. Schechem then sought honorably to marry her. Jacob left the matter in the hands of his sons, who falsely represented that they would agree, provided that every male in the city became circumcised. All able-bodied males in that city agreed and it was done. The following passage describes their trickery:

Then two days later, while they were still in great pain, Jacob's two sons Simeon and Levi, full brothers to Dinah, armed themselves with swords, boldly entered the city and killed every male. . . . They took Dinah from Schechem's house and went off with her. Then Jacob's other sons came in over the dead bodies and plundered the city, to avenge their sister's dishonor. They seized flocks, cattle, asses, and everything, both inside the city and outside in the open country; they also carried off all their possessions, their dependents, and their women, and plundered everything in the houses. . . .

Jacob, when he heard of this, was very worried about the bad impression it would make among other Canaanites. He required his sons to get rid of all the foreign gods they had among them (presumably idols taken as part of the booty) and moved his tents to a distant location.

This event would have taken place probably early in the seventeenth century B.C., but could not have been written down as history before the tenth century at the earliest. The historian cannot ignore the possibility (which, however, seems extremely unlikely) that it may have been invented later, for example, in the times of Ezra and Nehemiah, when every effort was being made to restore a strictly Jewish national consciousness. Some Jews who had returned to Jerusalem from Babylon were marrying Canaanite women and the story may have served to steel some Jewish hearts against all Canaanites. It is not a story to be proud of, except perhaps among the most intransigent and "hawkish" of Jewish fundamentalists. The fact that it was not softened or deleted at any point, especially not by Ezra in his definitive rendition of the Torah in 444 B.C., is in itself a historical fact of considerable interest.

The second element in the Covenant was Abraham's undertaking, for himself and his descendants, that they worship no other gods but God himself.

Abraham's pioneering selection of an abstract monotheism over the prevailing polytheism that made use of graven images appears, from this distance in history, as a matter of pure genius, without obvious sources. The mythology that has come down to us from earlier times (recorded in the earliest chapters of Genesis) did, as we have seen, postulate a single God. That tradition obviously had been lost among Abraham's contemporaries and even among his immediate family. The historian must register puzzlement as to how it happened to be born again, amidst general polytheism, in a form that could only have been written down 800 years later at the soonest by the scribes whose works eventually were brought together to form the Torah. Also why it reemerged in the form of an exclusive franchise between God and Abraham. One possible explanation, only slightly less unsatisfactory than others, would be that the God perceived by Abraham was indeed the God of the mythological period, Creator and Lord of *all* mankind, and that the exclusivity aspect was a later addition, in which case that feature would date most likely from the time of Moses.

Many centuries later, Isaiah and other late prophets modified this exclusivity feature. John the Baptist and Jesus of Nazareth rejected it, and after considerable hesitation, the small band of early Christians accepted the idea that God was for everybody. Muhammad most certainly espoused the universality of Allah's realm. Today, the population count of Christian and Muslim worshippers of God or Allah outnumbers that of the Jewish worshippers of Jahweh by about 150 to one.

A certain irony may be noted in passing. It lies in the scenario developed by Sigmund Freud, previously mentioned. He attributed Jewish monotheism to the work of an Egyptian Moses who had been passionately devoted to the monotheistic sun worship of Akhenaten. Another equally dubious tradition attributes Akhenaten's monotheism to the influence of a Jewish mother.

The third element in the Covenant, the "donation" by God of the land of Canaan to the children of Israel for them to occupy and rule forever, is most certainly of later origin, most likely at the time of Moses (with, as we have suggested, further embellishments by later scribes as the geopolitical fortunes and aspirations of the Jewish nation rose and fell). Abraham, Isaac, and Jacob led a pastoral-nomadic type of existence in which property ownership and formal sovereignty relationships were unknown, or at least for them, meaningless.

Abraham, Isaac, and Jacob successively had prospered greatly through intuitive skill in animal husbandry and doubtless also through an astute business sense in disposing of their produce. The caravan trade of that time would have provided favorable markets for pack animals, and they themselves may have participated in the caravan trade. Leather and wool made into clothing would have provided additional revenues. Isaac seems at one time to have been a successful grain farmer. Prosperity was equated with the power and the favor of one's gods, and in this regard, the God of Abraham manifestly did indeed keep special watch over Abraham, Isaac, and Jacob.

This pastoral-nomadic type of existence existed then and has existed down to modern times. It contrasts sharply with the more organized life-style of cities and states. The Bedouin families or tribes move their herds and flocks as necessary, in search of water and pasturage, into any lands they can find from which they will not be driven by superior force. Individual tribal groups tend to establish their own repetitive patterns of migration within certain areas, but this is without any formal sanction under any enforceable law. They also establish reputations for being good people or bad in accordance with their relations toward the more settled populations among whom they move. Until quite recent times in the Middle East, there has been adequate room for both the Bedouin types and the settled people, which is not to say that there has always been peace between them.

Abraham in his time seems to have owed his success not only to intuitive skill in animal husbandry and his astute sense of business practices, but also to his diplomacy. He made it a point, apparently, to be on good terms with the leaders of other pastoral-nomadic groups and with the rulers of the small city-states in the areas where his herds were pastured. He would not have been unaware that his considerable manpower (at one time his tribal group including immediate family, servants, herdsmen, and others comprised over 1,000 people) was a major factor in his security and his bargaining power. In an era when force was the only law, he sought rather to negotiate for whatever arrangements he desired. The point may be made in passing that this proclivity would have been a natural component, an active ingredient, in his pioneering religious nature.

A charming vignette illustrating Abraham's diplomacy, which is also a revealing documentation regarding property rights in general, and Abraham's status in particular, may be found at Genesis 23:1–20. Sarah, his half-sister and wife, mother of his son Isaac, had died, and he wished for a place to bury her.

Abraham was then encamped near Hebron. It seems to have been a sort of permanent camp, or a place to which he returned frequently if his life-style required seasonal migrations in search of pasture and water for his herds. Clearly he was well known and held in high honor by the more settled Hittite people then living in Hebron.[2] He was a well-behaved, pastoral nomad who knew their ways and respected their rights. Other nomadic leaders very likely were less well behaved, and the citizens of Hebron would therefore have regarded Abraham as welcome neighbor, ally, and protector.

Abraham approached the city, apparently at an hour when he knew that the elders would be gathered at the city gate, as was their custom. There he bowed before them and presented his petition: "I am an alien and settler among you. Give me land enough for a burial-place so that I can give my dead proper burial." The elders responded, "Do, pray, listen to what we have to say, sir. You are a mighty prince among us. Bury your dead in the best grave we have. There is not one of us who will deny you his grave or hinder you from burying your dead." Abraham stood up and then bowed low to the Hittites and requested them to speak to Ephron, son of Zohar, asking him to give the cave which belonged to him at Machpelah, but only in exchange for the full price, "so that I may take possession of it as a burial-place within your territory." Ephron happened to be sitting with the others (one suspects that Abraham knew that, but that the third-person approach was more diplomatic). He immediately gave Abraham what he asked: "In the presence of all my kinsmen, I give it to you. . . ." This appears to have been the sort of statement, which, spoken in the presence of the other elders, was (in those days, before written documents were common) as formal and binding as our modern elaborate ceremonial real estate "closings" in which surveys are recorded and evidence is submitted that title has been searched and found valid, followed by transfer of elaborately written deeds, etc.

Abraham bowed low before Ephron and said in their hearing, "If you really mean it, but do listen to me! I give you the price of the land, . . ." and Ephron said, "Do listen to me, sir, the land is worth four hundred shekels of silver. But what is that between you and me? There you may bury your dead." Thereupon Abraham came to an agreement with him and weighed out the amount that Ephron had named in the hearing of all the witnesses, 400 shekels of the standard recognized by merchants. Thus the plot, the cave that is on it and every tree on the plot, within the whole area, became the legal possession of Abraham, in the presence of all the Hittites as they came into the city gate. (Wording is that given in New English translation, Genesis 23:1–20.)

The historian must examine the quality of the sources. The account of this transaction with its meticulous legal formality, and the ceremonial courtesies that accompanied them, would have had to be passed along by word of mouth for at least seven or eight centuries before it could have been written down by the Hebrew scribes. Thus, the details of this story may have been reconstructed or invented at some later date by scribes familiar with later customary practice. However, customs would not have changed significantly. The event itself has every ring of authenticity. It is supported by later references to this same burial place on the occasions of Abraham's own burial there, Isaac's and Rebecca's, Jacob's and Leah's, and finally Joseph's.

Several details attract special interest. Abraham said of himself at the time that he was "an alien in the land and a settler there." His objective was to acquire legal title to a specific plot in a land where, up to that time, he had owned none. His status would have been comparable to that of the Bedouin described above, making no pretense to ownership of the land they used but feeling free to use any land from which they were not driven by force.

We pause to note the striking contrast between this picture of a good-neighbor relationship between the pastoral-nomadic chieftain and agricultural-commercial city-state, and that of the bad-neighbor relationship between the children of Israel (Abraham's great-grandchildren) set forth in the story of Dinah mentioned above; one story is so creditable and the other so discreditable. Yet both are faithfully recorded in the same document.

Neither Abraham himself, nor Isaac nor Jacob—who also prospered greatly through utilizing lands that they occupied in the age-old manner of pastoral nomads—would be likely to have received a revelation to change that arrangement. That would however have occurred after perhaps four centuries of living in Egypt under totally different social, economic, and political circumstances, when the children of Israel, now greatly increased in numbers, and long habituated to the settled agricultural life of Egypt, came to be reduced to very near the status of slavery. Under those circumstances they may well have begun to long for land of their own to occupy and rule.

Only at this time and no sooner, in our scenario, would a "revela-

tion" that the Lord intended them to occupy and rule the land of
Canaan make sense. It then would be, as the saying goes, "a natural." This dating fits in with the usually accepted dates for Moses
and the Exodus. It would have been three centuries or longer after
the 1567 B.C. fall of the Hyksos, the "shepherd kings from the East."
During that long period, most glorious for Egypt, the Israelites seem
not to have been intensely unhappy. Had they been so, they could
have filtered back to the east and taken up a pastoral-nomadic existence in small groups. That option apparently was not attractive to
them despite their deteriorating political and social status. Or, without Moses's vision and leadership it had not yet come to mind.

We must again face the question as to which stories from the
patriarchal period were preserved intact, which are authentically old
but were altered and embellished in the course of innumerable retell-
ings, and which represent pious fiction. No history of their sojourn
in Egypt has been preserved. Was it deliberately suppressed? What
changes in Jewish cultural values and sense of tribal togetherness,
religion, and life-style had occurred as a result of Egyptian influences? Did the Jews have any sense of being a "chosen" people
before Moses? To what extent did Moses rekindle an old fire or to
what extent did he ignite a new one? Did he invent a religious
"tradition" as well as a national identity and sense of destiny?

Our theory as developed above may be summarized as follows:
the alleged divine donation of the land of Canaan to the children of
Israel was introduced in Moses's time; it was unknown and un-
thinkable in Abraham's time. For Moses it was the obvious solution
to an obvious problem. Except for Kamal Salibi's untested theory
that the Jewish nation came originally from Asir in Saudi Arabia,
the Israelites' distant ancestors had by general consent pastured their
flocks in the land of Canaan. Also—much more important—Canaan
at that time was the only possible destination that they could aspire
to attain beyond the reach of Egyptian whips. They had no ships.
The land alternatives to an Exodus northeastward would have been
(a) to the south along the length of the Nile valley toward Sudan and
Ethiopia, or (b) to the west across 120 miles or more of Nile delta,
with its network of "mouths" and interconnecting canals, swampy
places, and densely populated areas; then along the coastal road
toward Libya.

Nearly everybody likes to feel morally justified whatever they do, particularly in an act of aggression—Jewish people no less than others. It would have been an important morale booster for the invaders to believe that God had given them the land they wished to take, and that they were fighting on God's side, doing what he had commanded, as they proceeded to slaughter its occupants.

Other later periods in Jewish history also provide historical circumstances in which the divine donation idea would have been useful to support the zeal of the Israeli fighting forces. These also would have been times when the story about a divine revelation might have been invented, or further embellished if already in existence. Israel's great warrior-king and poet, David (ruled ca. 1012–972 B.C.), had succeeded in throwing off Israelite vassalage to the Philistines and, in fact, had reversed that relationship. He also carried on incessant warfare against his neighbors to the east and south, extending the boundaries of his domain in those directions. Many of the tribes then living in the way of his ambitions were traditional descendants of Ishmael and/or of Abraham's later sons by different wives, or of Esau (Edom).

These tribes, unlike the hated Canaanites, were children of Abraham and thus distant cousins of the children of Israel. By quoting the Lord as having specifically excluded all these distant cousins from the Covenant and adding the gratuitous detail that Esau had been condemned by Isaac to serve his brother, the Israelites would feel morally justified in their wars of conquest. They had already carried out the will of the Lord by taking possession of the land of Canaan. The expansion of their boundaries into their cousins' territory simply confirmed that they had thereby earned the Lord's good will; he was rewarding them by extending the boundaries of his promise.

There are several versions of this donation. In one, the donation extended from the Nile to the Euphrates (Genesis 15:18). In the version recorded at Numbers 34:1–2, the boundaries were defined in meticulous detail, but were less extensive. The Nile-to-Euphrates version of the "donation" would have seemed more realistically achievable, and would have been more valuable as a tonic for the army's morale, during the golden era under Kings David and Solomon, than at any other time in Jewish history.

Revelation is a form of religious experience, but it also was an extremely useful medium through which a wise legislator, deeply committed to the welfare of his people (a category in which one must unhesitatingly place Moses, Muhammad, and many other prophets), can gain acceptance and conformance for his proposals. Thus we postulate total sincerity on the part of Moses, Muhammad, and the others when they produced the messages which they had received, they thought, as the voice of the Lord telling them what, we believe, they secretly or unconsciously wanted to hear. Among the people of their time—superstitious, uneducated, stiff-necked, fiercely independent—the fear of a terrible spirit looking down from somewhere "up there," and of retribution in a future life, made any message put forward as revelation (which is to say as Word of God) enormously effective. It was the only way to get the message across.

The position of Christ in this world of revelation is somewhat different. The three synoptic Gospels all report the same incident: he had spoken at the synagogue in Capernaum and "the people were astounded at his teaching for, unlike the doctors of the law, he taught with a note of authority." Whereas Moses before him and Muhammad afterwards transmitted specific Law for mankind's guidance and obedience, laid down by a distant and fear-inspiring God, based on revelations which they alone were privileged to hear, Christ spoke on his own authority of an inner spirit which everyone might share, which humanized the application of the Law.

We have mentioned his selection of the father-simile to explain the nature of God as he perceived it: a kindly, wise, forgiving, heavenly father, to be trusted and loved in the way a young child would trust and love its worldly father. This concept is woven into the concept of a Kingdom of Heaven which may exist within people's minds and hearts here, now, in this life, and of course is promised for the next life: "In my father's house are many mansions," and so forth.

Christ had no end of trouble during his lifetime in putting these revolutionary ideas across. Nobody seems to have understood the essential identity and interchangeability of his roles as son of man and son of God. The first was as an ordinary fellow human being— albeit in his case one endowed with unique and superlative intellectual and spiritual faculties. The second was still as an ordinary human but one who was totally committed to and wrapped up in the Kingdom of Heaven concept. One suspects that many of even his most devoted followers were devoted more because of the charisma of his personality than as a result of understanding and embracing

the spiritual concept so clearly embodied in what we call the Lord's
Prayer:

> *Our* Father in heaven,
> thy name be hallowed;
> thy kingdom come
> thy will be done,
> *on earth* as it is in heaven
>
> (New English translation, 1970; author's italics)

followed by a simple asking for enough to eat today (no thought for
the morrow), for forgiveness contingent on a spirit of forgiving, and
then those enigmatic lines, which the New English translators have
given as follows:

> And do not bring us to the test,
> but save us from the evil one.

This exceedingly simple list of wants, linked to the example set by
Christ's own exceedingly simple lifestyle, creates a question which
we shall not try to answer: what degree of austerity in life-style did
Christ think necessary to qualify for admission to the Kingdom of
Heaven—in this world or the next. One clue would be the story
(Matthew 19:16–26) which contains the statement: "A rich man will
find it hard (note—not specifically impossible) to enter the kingdom
of heaven." Then, in response to the disciples' puzzlement over the
simile about the camel passing through the needle's eye, his enigmatic statement: "For men this is impossible; but everything is possible
for God."

History records a major movement, beginning probably in the
late first century A.D. but reaching historic proportions in the fourth
and fifth centuries, of people seeking to qualify for the Kingdom of
Heaven through self-denial, often in ways we would regard as at
least bizarre, sometimes repulsive. St. Simeon Stylites, possibly the
most colorful example, spent 35 years on his pillar in the mountains
east of Latakia in Syria (the exact location is called Kalaat-El-Moudik
on the *Freytag-Berndt Road Map of the Middle East* and Seleucobelus in
Atlas Antiquus—places unknown to the modern *Lippincott's Gazeteer*
or *The (London) Times Atlas of the World*). Simeon became a major

tourist attraction in his day (d. ca. A.D. 459). Others, probably to be counted in thousands and more likely in tens of thousands at any one time, lived as anchorites, eremites, hermits, in rocky caves or crude huts under extreme climatic conditions in the Nile valley and the mountains and deserts of Palestine and Syria. The movement extended in medieval times also to Europe. The monastic movement pursued somewhat parallel objectives, but often combined these with more constructive and socially useful practices. If, as we believe, the Kingdom of Heaven was a state of mind rather than a set of rules, who can judge the efficacy of these harsh measures to achieve it?

Our quest from the beginning has been for convincing answers to such questions as: Why do all groups of human beings have some sort of religious system? Why are the systems so different? What good or bad do they do? Is there any "right" or "wrong" system?

Some answers have emerged. It seems fairly well established that an original man was not designed or put together from scratch by some anthropomorphic master craftsman. Human beings emerged as an evolutionary product through an almost infinite number of mutations on a hit-or-miss basis, some of which survived the natural selection processes. In the course of this development, humans were genetically endowed with—along with many other special endowments—a most remarkable brain. That much is hardly controversial. We argue that one property of the human brain is the capability and compulsion for religious thought. People are religious animals.

As do so many other genetic characteristics of *Homo sapiens* vary widely from individual to individual and group to group, so does religious quotient. Some difference may be due to genetic physiological differences in the composition and arrangements of neurons within different brains. More differences would be traced to environmental factors, some beyond the control of the individual person, but many within our control—education, motivation, and the like. In any group there would be some to act as starters and the others are preprogrammed to come along.

When we take up the question, what good or bad do these systems do, we have come back close to our question about Christ's own intent when he enunciated the Kingdom of Heaven concept (with which we associated closely the Holy Spirit concept). Our theory argues that there is a necessary connection between the physical and spiritual well-being of man. The connection is not a matter of theology but of common sense. What constitutes well-being and whether it is to be viewed as an immediate or long-term objective are topics for separate discussion.

Thoughtful reading of the Gospel accounts leads to the conclusion that Christ's own time horizon was *very* short: today, here, now, no thought for the morrow. One would hope in the interest of future humanity that the same or similar humanitarian Christian principles can be preserved and applied beneficially even though the time horizons were to be moved farther out—much farther out.

Modern business management has developed a complex computerized management tool called the input-output chart, intended to show what repercussions will occur throughout an organization if a change is made in one of the parts. The idea is that the sum total of results from any decision must, on balance, be favorable even though the effect in some places would be negative. This technique is very far from perfect, but the concept is useful for our purpose. It introduces recognition of the fact that an action motivated by Christian kindness to one person in one place, effective as of now, may (though this would be an extreme example) prove harshly cruel for other people elsewhere, or might have bad effects which would linger on for years. In this vein, human well-being now may be in conflict with long-term survival here on Earth. At issue are questions, answers to which depend on wise and, therefore in the long run, humane decisions in matters such as population control and all the correlated ecological and natural resource problems. Religious impulses springing from the heart (or, to be scientific about it, from certain parts of the brain) must be coordinated with long-range planning for the well-being of humanity and these two must be developed synergistically though perhaps coming from different parts of the human brain.

We return to the discussion of Christ's role in a world of revelation. He did not directly attack religious law as revealed to Moses, nor the civil law as imposed by Caesar. His "revelation" was that all law and all human relationships should be conducted in a manner sensitive to real needs and with humane compassion. This he illustrated in many parables, and by many actions. That sensitivity and compassion was communicated to human beings as part of a mysterious force—built into the human psyche, we think, but coming from somewhere "out there" he thought—constantly providing guidance and motivation. This force (the Holy Spirit) may have had other manifestations but common sense sensitivity to real needs and humane compassion were essentials—sine qua non.

The source of this force was a God whom he perceived as a kindly, forgiving, but still no-nonsense sort of authority figure, and whom he insisted on calling my Father. The Spirit was in fact a reflection of that image. His insistence on that terminology caused no end of trouble. To the Pharisees it was a profanation of deity and worthy of death. For his followers who believed it literally, it created the necessity of inventing the myth of virgin birth. One puzzles whether this insistence was simple naiveté on his part (as the response to it was certainly intellectual dullness on the others' part), or whether he welcomed the confrontation as a part of his mission.

NOTES

1. Ages in the biblical accounts require modification. There is no reason to suppose that the human animal was physiologically longer-lived in mythical and legendary times than today, although environmental and dietary conditions would then, as now, extend or shorten human life spans individually and as groups. Doubtless, then as now, some families would have been noted for longer living individuals.

Ages are meticulously recorded for the mythological and legendary characters. As a very rough rule of thumb, the ages given for the mythological forebears (Adam through Noah, and including Methuselah) may be divided by a factor of 10 to bring them within reasonable human expectancy, and the ages given for the legendary patriarchs (Abraham through Moses) by a factor of two. Thus, Sarah would have been 45 years old—close to the end of her childbearing years, but not beyond, when Isaac was born.

The same numerical factors seem not to apply to other biblical statements involving the passage of time. As to the question whether Abraham's decision to undergo circumcision had any connection with Sarah's pregnancy, the historian must step aside and leave that discussion to the gynecologist. There is no reason to question the assumption that Sarah underwent the usual nine-month pregnancy, which according to biblical record would have begun three months after Abraham had been circumcised.

2. These Hittites are thought to have been a small tribe of Semitic people who occupied Hebron and its adjacent territory at this time (probably eighteenth to seventeenth century B.C.), but were no relation to the Indo-European Hittites who were entering into Cappadocia (modern East-Central

Turkey, ca. 1800 B.C.). The latter, of course, became an important factor in the history of the region, marked by the Old Hittite Kingdom (1600–1400 B.C.) and the Hittite Empire (1400–1200 B.C.), followed by a period of smaller city-states with Hittite rulers and a neo-Hittite kingdom (ca. 1050–700 B.C.). The latter was finally destroyed by the Assyrians at about the same time that the latter captured and destroyed the northern ten tribes of Israel.

Although Abraham had been on good terms with the local Hittites, they were on Moses' hit list. Speaking to him amid thunder and lightning, smoke, and trumpet sound on Mount Sinai, in the wilderness, the Lord said:

> . . . I will be an ememy to your enemies, and I will harrass those who harrass you. My angel will go before you and bring you to the Amorites, the Hittites, . . . and I will make an end of them. . . .
>
> Exodus 23:20–33

The Hittite name, referring presumably to this small Semitic tribe and not to the Indo-European nation, appears again in King David's time (ca. 1013–973 B.C.) at least seven centuries after the time of Abraham. In the latter instance, Uriah the Hittite appears as a brave and upright soldier, the grievously wronged husband of Bathsheba, who later became mother of Solomon (2 Samuel 11:1–27). The fact that David had ruled first from Hebron suggests that this Uriah had joined his service there, and that there was still a distinct tribe of that name in the area.

11   Did He Who Made the Lamb
Make Thee?

"Yes!" says modern scientific man, "No question about it!" However, this answer is put forward in accordance with scientific understandings that would not have been possible when Blake shaped the question. These understandings are as follows:

"He who" (the ultimate maker) would be Deus Universalis: the impersonal, unthinking, unplanning, unfeeling, but ongoing energy by which the universe was formed and which is the essence of all matter in every form, and of all natural forces (gravity, electricity, light and so forth). This force led long ago to the synthesis of life on Earth, and to its diversification and multiplication through the evolutionary process to produce all living things, each with its special characteristics. However different two organisms may be, both necessarily had the same ultimate maker.

The word "made," however, implies anthropomorphic planning and thinking. This can only be done with a physical human-type brain made up of neurons, neurotransmitters and a central nervous system to bring in the stimuli and carry away instructions to muscles that will put thoughts into action. This requires physical matter: special molecules very specifically arranged. The primordial force to which we refer as Deus Universalis does not work that way. Instead of the word "made," we would prefer to use the word "caused."

In explanation and defense of the foregoing, the scientist would say: What was before the big bang man does not know, though there are speculative theories. Thus the word "made," implying a creative act, must be used with care. Starting with the big bang, matter as we know it came into being, impelled by enormous energy. It has been in motion ever since. In the course of unimaginably many trillions of trillions of happenings—happenings which occurred in accordance with the combined predictable effects of the natural laws of physics and the unpredictable incidence of random chance—the universe has taken the shape that we can observe. Some of those happenings produced Earth, and on Earth synthesized life, and out of life produced through a series of evolutionary mutations, all of the plant and animal forms that have covered Earth as we know it. Each has its own characteristics but the same process produced them all. Poetically, all are children of the same father.

Certainly the "maker" (Blake's word, to which we attach a very different connotation) did *not* smile his work to see. He (more correctly "it") had no anthropomorphic motivations, performed no anthropomorphic handiwork, and felt no anthropomorphic emotions whatsoever.

Blake's imagery concentrates on two extremes, one evoking fear and terror in the human heart and mind, the other indescribable feelings of love, peace, and security. As mentioned before, we cannot be completely sure exactly what Blake had in mind when he wrote this poem. Was it a real tyger prowling about in the forests of the night (which is terrible enough to think about even though he and we are not personally threatened)? Or was he thinking symbolically of the savage predator which lurks among the psychic characteristics observable in the human race? And were his "forests of the night" really in India or symbolic of the hard core ignorance, prejudice, racism, bigotry, etc., with which we are always surrounded, in London two centuries ago and in New York today?

Let us first say a few words on tyger's behalf. As symbol, he is ruthless power, savagery, all the more terrifying because he will spring out of the dark unexpectedly upon some defenseless victim. But as a real animal he is not such a bad fellow. He has to eat. Springing out of the dark on unsuspecting victims is the way he performs what is to him a necessary chore. So far as we know, he does not act out of any inherent malice toward any particular victim, but of course he *is* devoid of compassion. Tygers are (we presume) generically devoid of both malice and compassion. At least Blake's tyger was. Human beings generically possess both as part of their psychic makeup. There is not all that much difference zoologically between tyger and the familiar well-loved house cat—no difference except size and habitat. One has the impression that tyger's characteristics as parent are probably rather superior to those of house cat: that both tyger parents are loving, attentive, and providing parents, at least until the cubs are big enough to compete.

Blake's figure, the Lamb, symbolizes Jesus of Nazareth, of whom we have spoken at length in previous chapters. It is very clear that Blake's own images regarding Jesus would be quite different from what we respectfully regard as the medically and historically more realistic picture presented here, in previous chapters. Blake could not have been more adoring of his image than we are admiring of ours. Be that as it may, the Lamb is symbolic of a special formulation of beliefs set forth in the Christian Gospels for all to read, and for each to interpret in accordance with his or her own viewpoint. In our view, they are deeply rooted in Biblical tradition, a composite of conscience, moral and ethical principles, forgiveness (the Jewish ethos being heavily burdened with sense of guilt), compassion, and good will toward fellow man, guided and motivated by the Holy Spirit. This latter, a term which means different things to different people, seems to have meant to Christ more than channel of communication: a sort of participating interest, constantly renewed, in the wisdom and compassion of his Heavenly Father—the latter a spiritual concept utilizing the word Father only because there was no other to describe a relationship closely comparable to the relationship of a small child with its wise and kindly worldly father which would have had any meaning to his hearers. Much of his teaching was carried out by means of parables beginning: "The Kingdom of Heaven is like . . . " (followed by some worldly situation which would have meaning to his hearers); so, the relationship with God is like . . . (followed by "father").

Perhaps the simplest presentation of the allegory created by Blake's poetic question: "Did he who made the Lamb make thee?" (to which we have answered unequivocally, "Yes") is to present a pro forma human being with two natures, one all animal, savage, rapacious and the other spiritual, moral, loving, each struggling for supremacy over the other. In real life, people are much more complex. They have a greater variety of natures than that, and the natures often blend into each other. The historian is confronted repeatedly with records of atrocities carried out in the name of the Prince of Peace (a name which military people and their allies seem to prefer over "the Lamb" as a designation for Jesus of Nazareth). Still it is necessary to see in tyger and Lamb symbols of distinctive aspects of human nature. One has long cherished far at the back of one's mind the thought that life on Earth would be ever so much better if "the Lamb" could participate to a much greater degree in the decisions which affect our lives, decisions which we ourselves make and decisions made by others that restrict our freedom or in some cases open opportunities we could not secure for ourselves.

What kind of decisions are we talking about? Whether or not to give money to the beggar in the subway—and how much? Whether to hate or forgive the meter maid who didn't really have to give us a ticket for that extra minute of parking, but did? Making the choice between a sacrificial contribution to some badly needed charitable cause or some selfish expenditure: taking one's wife to dinner and theater or buying a yacht? Whether to evict—in mid winter—the last intractable squatters, a handful of weeping, abusive, minority families, from a large unheated, dangerously dilapidated tenement block overdue to be torn down and replaced with a new multi-million-dollar state-of-the-art home and hospital for the aged, or to order the heat turned on? It is not frivolous to say that Holy Spirit (in our definition of that term) is present, and its guidance accepted or rejected, in every one of these decisions—and in 10,000 more!

What is the time-horizon on Holy Spirit? For the Lamb, it was, or seems to us to have been as discussed above, extremely short: today, here, now. Give no thought for the morrow; the morrow will take care of itself. But it is absolutely essential, if human life is to continue on this planet Earth, that we do give serious thought to the morrows. To that extent, and in that context only, one must question whether life on Earth really would be all that much better for everybody or anybody if the Lamb and his modern followers did have complete responsibility.

Within the last few years, relatively speaking (4–5 milliseconds on our 6-day scale), the enormously superior physical and intellectual advantages of *Homo sapiens* have asserted themselves to the point of completely unbalancing all natural selection–survival of the fittest equations. The human race is now its own worst and only real enemy. Medical sciences, agricultural sciences, mineral sciences, mechanical inventions, transportation and distribution systems, etc., have combined to make available previously unimaginable improvements in life-style for hundreds of millions of people. But simultaneously they have created conditions whereby several billions have been added to our global population, many condemned to live at sub-subsistence levels of diet, often under inhuman political conditions. Fossil fuels make people mobile and provide electricity for their homes, hospitals, and factories, but threaten their health and perhaps worse, through atmospheric pollution and in other ways. Natural resources are abundant but not inexhaustible. Nuclear energy solves many pollution problems but creates others.

The technology which has created these problems carries with it the hope for technology to solve them. If our leaders—scientists, industrialists, politicians, chairmen of the thousands of influential committees—will adopt wise, far-seeing decisions, there is an extraordinarily bright hope for *Homo sapiens*. If not, he will slowly strangle himself, through overpopulation and its consequences, or end it all in nuclear holocaust or experience some dire combination of the two. What will guide and motivate him in right directions? The Lamb? Our inquiries have raised unexpected doubts. Selfless love and compassion toward fellow man, giving all one has to help him (a crude approximation of the worldly aspects of Holy Spirit as defined here) are seen already hard at work in the many state and private organizations dedicated to feeding the hungry, providing clothing and shelter for those who need it, and seeking to ameliorate the condition of the disadvantaged in many other ways. These do not attack problems at their root. In medical terms, palliative measures may provide a moment of relief but do nothing to cure, and in some cases may even exacerbate the underlying disease.

Our question, implicit throughout this work and explicit three paragraphs above, therefore more or less answers itself. That aspect of human nature symbolized by the Lamb cannot and should not be expected to take charge—and certainly that aspect symbolized by tyger must not be allowed to take charge. Neither of these two could control the other or find common ground to work together. We must look elsewhere. There are other aspects to human nature. The one which matters most in the development of our thesis was symbolized in Christ's time by the word "Caesar." We should prefer some other word more suggestive of democratic government responsive to an enlightened and forward-looking electorate.

Christ's concept of a Kingdom of Heaven holding sway in the

hearts and minds of living people could only exist under the umbrella of a government such as that provided by the Roman imperium: a system of laws wisely drawn and on balance fairly administered, a civil administration to regulate an orderly economic infrastructure including roads, bridges, etc., able to support a large and on balance prosperous population, and finally a military presence which held off raiding Bedouin tribesmen and the armies of hostile aggressors from the East. To the Pharisees and Zealots of Christ's time this was "oppression"; to Christ it was freedom.

"Render unto Caesar the things that are Caesar's, and unto God, the things that are God's." The principle of dual responsibility, one toward Caesar and one toward God, is still useful though we would supply different symbolism. The Kingdom of Heaven concept is now seen as having its seat in the innate religiosity of the human brain, and the more worldly survival of the species concept as having its seat in some other compartment of the same. The Kingdom of Heaven concept has a time-horizon of now, here. The survival of the species concept has a time-horizon extending many centuries and is global. Without human existence, neither concept would exist; ways must be found to make them work more closely together, each to strengthen and enrich the other.

12   Summary

The stated objective of our present work has been to answer William
Blake's poetical question: "Did he who made the Lamb make thee
(tyger)?" It is a good question. One is glad Blake asked it, but the
process of answering has carried us far beyond anything Blake could
have had in mind when he wrote that poem. To continue with his
symbolic imagery, we hope to have made a valid contribution toward the objective of leading people out of "the forests of the night"
(symbolic of ignorance, superstition, bigotry), toward socially and
spiritually useful knowledge, understanding and the goodwill which
can prevail where bigotry is absent. This quest has involved presentation of some new perceptions and new perspectives relative to
human beings' age-old questions: Who are we? How did we get
here? What is the purpose of our being here? What are the rules of
the game? And now a new question: How long can we (*Homo sapiens*)
survive here on this planet Earth?

All of us should ask these questions and take a lively interest in the
answers. They involve the well-being of individuals and of the
human race. The term "well-being" is one of those troublesome
terms which means different things to different people. Does it
mean: "just me and my immediate circle of family and friends, here,
now?" Or does it mean: "all human beings who may be living any-
time in the future anywhere on this globe?" Does it mean living
under conditions where all have freedom to enjoy the good things of
life, or does it mean merely being alive and able to eke out just the

basic necessities of life on a grossly overpopulated, exhausted, polluted planet?

All of these questions, and more like them, must be freshly asked and the answers formulated in light of information which did not exist in Blake's day, and certainly did not exist when the doctrinaire answers which he and we have been given were formulated. The scientific era (Bacon 1620, Newton 1687, Darwin 1859, Hubble 1929) has carried mankind past a sort of intellectual watershed. People are slow to appreciate that fact. They have refrigerators, automobiles, airplanes, computers, miracle drugs, leisure, and comforts that could not have been dreamed of even 200 years ago; yet many people adhere to a cosmology built on philosophical speculation and pious intuition promulgated as divine revelation, and unquestioning acceptance of the wisdom and authority of sacred scripture.

The old cosmology was formulated by gifted intellects around simple observations of stars wheeling overhead in the night sky, sun and moon rising and setting, weather phenomena, the birth-death cycle, and so forth. The scientific era has brought us a new cosmology built on findings certainly in the physical sciences but also in the social sciences arrived at through an entirely new methodology, and producing a virtual explosion of new information on a very great variety of subjects.

We have been particularly interested in the findings and new theories about the formation of our universe (in a big bang) and its subsequent development driven by blind, impersonal, universal, all-pervasive energy—an energy manifest in the movement of stars and galaxies but also in the smallest particles of matter. The synthesis of life on Earth is seen as one specialized manifestation of this universal energy, and our species as one unique product of the evolutionary process which began with synthesis of life. With the emergence of man onto the cosmic stage came awareness of deity. Naturally enough, since people had no other pattern to utilize in formulating their images of the deity, the images that they conceived were given anthropomorphic attributes.

We think it necessary to realize and accept the fact that such images have their origin in the mind of man and have no existence apart from the mind of man. There are important consequences to that recognition, which we regard as beneficial or even in the long run essential for the well-being and survival of the human race—lest

we be led into narrowly self-serving and in the long run self-destruc-
tive courses of action under a false illusion that they conform with
eternal immutable commands "revealed" from on high and carrying
suprahuman wisdom and authority.

As man is a scientifically verifiable reality, the working of his
mind is an as yet little understood scientifically verifiable reality.
Man's religious nature is a part of that reality. However, these so-
called revelations are not scientifically or historically verifiable except as statements of one or another highly gifted human being who,
as the historians amongst us can demonstrate, usually had a particular axe to grind.

One might describe the human mind as the last great frontier for
scientific discovery, at least for now. It is an instrument which has
given people truly extraordinary powers to adapt to their environment and to overcome forces that threaten. It is the seat of all human
thoughts, feelings, hopes, fears, moral instincts, religious aspirations, and much more. The neurosciences have made enormous
strides, mostly within the last few years, opening doors toward a
beginning of understanding of the human brain's physiological characteristics and how it works—the "hardware," if one may borrow
computer language, for an instrument that far surpasses in complexity and range any electronic computer which the human brain has
yet devised. How it gets its "software," and what finite possibilities
and limitations there are as to an individual's own personal control
over his own brain's input and output are matters of greatest interest, but as yet beyond the horizons of the amateur science-
watcher.

It is not too much to hope that scientific knowledge will identify
more and more areas of human behavior as resulting from specific
manageable conditions in the brain. This kind of knowledge may
help combat drug addiction, Alzheimer's syndrome, and other debilitating human afflictions. The idea that science may find ways to
control human behavior, human thought, or human genetics, however, causes deep dismay in many minds. This dismay arises from
fears that this knowledge and power will be used to aggrandize its
possessor and debase others. At the same time others find in this
prospect great hope, based upon the good this knowledge may do.

This as yet unrealized, or only partially realized, promise of vastly
greater knowledge and understanding about the physiological func-

tioning of the brain, with every indication that those functions (some of them at any rate), will respond to human ministrations, carries with it enormous responsibility. That knowledge and the power that it confers must be (or at least we must do everything in our power to make sure that it is) exercised in the manner in which a wise, kindly, forgiving, loving human father would behave toward his young dependent children. To employ once more the imagery of Blake's poem, we must look to those aspects of human nature symbolized by the Lamb and find ways to protect ourselves from those symbolized by the tyger.

Beyond that we must be on guard against a certain "improvidence" which we have detected as inherent in the humane qualities identified with the Lamb: a very short time-horizon limited to the here and now with no thought given for the morrow; the morrow must take care of itself. In the cosmology which we advocate care for the morrow and many morrows after that is exceedingly important. Perhaps "exceedingly" is not a strong enough word to use here: it is essential for the survival and well-being of our species.

Lest we grow too serious in pursuit of this point let us also remind ourselves of a story reported by Voltaire (*Oeuvres Completes*, xlviii, 99): The Abbé Desfontaines had been brought before the Count d'Argenson (apparently a senior magistrate) for publishing libels, and excused himself by saying, "After all, I must live." The Count d'Argenson responded, "I do not see the necessity of that." The incisive barb is perhaps a little sharper if the story is told in French and might be even sharper if we knew more about the personalities and backgrounds of the Abbé and the Count. Nevertheless the point has been made and we hope will not be lost on the posterity for whose well-being we are expressing such great concern.

The lovable, trusting, young children—whose relationship with their wise, compassionate, forgiving, providing worldly fathers presents such an ideal model in the symbolism used by Christ—present one major problem; they grow up! We must regard each successive generation of children growing up and coming into the body politic as no less dangerous to our way of life than the waves of Goths and Huns and Vandals which swept over western Europe in the fourth and fifth centuries A.D. were to the Roman Empire. In our situation the defenses comprise, not armies and geographical barriers, and certainly not nuclear holocaust, but schools and all other educational media. We must see to it that our way of life, not a static way but one responsive to well-considered improvements, is worth continuing and that the newcomers are persuaded to that effect. In Roman Empire days, an infusion of vigorous new blood from outside was welcomed and was beneficial, but uncontrollable waves of uneducable barbarians uneducable through sheer numbers and time limitations set in motion the downward spiral which culminated in the dark ages of the ninth and tenth centuries. So in our days the world population explosion is the most dangerous social phenomenon with which we have to deal.

Whatever the future holds for humankind, people have only themselves to look to for guidance, motivation, and restraint. To the extent that choices can be made (and simply drifting along is in itself one sort of choice), no help will come from some benign abstract spirit residing vaguely "up there." To be sure, there is an enormously important something "up there," and "out there," and everywhere: a universal energy and dynamism that is the vitality and essence of the universe, a vitality which ensures change. It is a totally impersonal, purposeless, inexorable force—no friends, no enemies. Human beings alone, so far as we know, are the only agents to have appeared anywhere in the cosmic scheme of things who have intellectual equipment and physical means to impart direction. Humans can, to a very limited extent as yet, master some of this energy as manifested for example in electricity, gravity, and other intangible forces and of course in all available materials (matter is simply organized energy). We have called that force Deus Universalis.

The selection by human beings of purposes to which this force can and should be applied is another matter. Sometimes the purposes seem purely practical but, as humans are innately religious animals (without any design on the part of Deus Universalis—they just turned out that way), they do establish moral and spiritual values, and it's a good thing they do. Those values do not come from abstract beings floating around "out there," but from some as yet totally mysterious physiological compositions, arrangement, and pattern of activity of special neurons with their remarkable chemical and electric activities, "in here."

The reader is reminded that alleged messages from the imagined "God up there" have been used directly to incite or indirectly to justify inhuman actions which common sense and humane compassion now deplore: Jewish slaughter of Canaanites during the original occupation of the land of Canaan, innumerable Christian persecutions of heretics culminating in the Spanish Inquisition, many ruthless acts of the Crusaders (more against Jews than Muslims), the Arab Conquests, Muslim bloodshed over divine right to rule and over many other issues culminating in the terrors of a Qaddafi regime or Khomeini's attempts at thought control, oppressions by theocratic fundamentalists in all three major branches of the Semitic "revealed" religions: Pharisees, conservative theologians, and "ulama." That list of acts of aggression and oppression carried out in the name of religion is long, but alleviated, of course, by equally many or more unnoticed acts of kindness and compassion (wise and unwise), often quite self-sacrificing, seeking no reward, performed by different people under the same religious auspices, or even by the same people under different circumstances.

The point is that human behavior under the supposed guidance and control of "God up there" has been nothing to boast about. One may hope that it will at least be no worse when the "God in here" concept is fully established and supported by awareness of the increasing urgency to make wise as well as compassionate decisions affecting not only fellow human beings here and now, but others far into the future.

The speed with which new scientific discoveries are being made, and new hypotheses as to what conclusions one may draw from a given series of discoveries, seems to be accelerating at an accelerating rate. It is confusing. Perhaps this factor is at least partly to blame for the reappearance or reassertiveness of religious fundamentalism, equally in Judaism, Christianity, and Islam. People need faith. Ordinary people throw up their hands and ask without hope of a satisfactory answer: What *can* I believe! The fundamentalists are right there with absolute assurance: "Believe this!" Those who have been adrift find anchorage. Others take comfort in reaffirming the old familiar ways.

It has been said that religious beliefs are last to change in a changing society. R. W. Bulliet of Columbia University has shown in his *Conversion to Islam in the Medieval Period* that it required about 400 years for the population in countries conquered by the Arabs to become completely converted to Islam, mostly from Christianity but also from Zoroastrianism and some Buddhism. At the end of the first 100 years less than 10 percent had converted. (Islam was founded A.D. 622; the greatest conquests were completed by approximately 650 and by 750 Islam had established its sovereignty from Agadir and the Pyrenees to the Indus and the borders of China.) After 300 years, 90 percent had converted. It required the final 100 years for the last die-hards to come over. Contrary to popular impression, the sword was a negligible factor in conversion; conversion through well-considered changes in theological conviction was probably not much greater as a factor. Economic and legal reasons were quite persuasive (dhimmis paid a special tax and were at a disadvantage under the shari'a legal system). Just getting used to the idea was probably the major factor.

One sees the same human reaction against "progress" in evidence from time to time when an old building is threatened with demolition; a committee is formed to saved it. Housewives place themselves with baby carriages in front of the bulldozers. Our society loves to preserve old things: buildings, even whole neighborhoods, as nostalgic reminders of a past whose discomforts have been forgotten.

In one light, this stubborn adhesion to old beliefs is harmless and even beneficial to the individuals involved—so long as it affects only their own lives, and that of kindred spirits. Old faith acts for them as a sort of balance wheel or, to change the metaphor, as a secure haven in time of storm and stress. From another point of view, however, it is not at all harmless. Through political action committees, through evangelical "empires" on radio and TV, through occasional mob terrorism, and through "fellow travelers" who occupy key posts in government administration and judiciary, they condemn the body politic to streaks of regressive and bigoted legislation, and occasionally to outrageous foreign policy. We refer here, of course, to anti-abortion laws and to court decisions of the same genre, which condemn penniless and socially insecure women to bear unwanted children for whom there is no hope of love or security—a cruelty to the victims and a cancer in an otherwise generally humane and enlightened society.

We refer to legislative or administrative decisions which deny foreign aid to countries and to organizations working in those countries where the cause of population control is at issue. It is seemingly a religious question of "human rights" as between the right of an unwanted fetus to be born into a world where the population explosion itself, and the whole family of related ecological, economic, and public health problems are more real and pressing than even the nuclear holocaust problem—versus the right of humane and enlightened societies to take measures necessary to preserve the quality of life where it is tolerable and improve it where it is intolerable. In this case "human rights" as here interpreted and "humaneness" are in direct conflict with one another.

We refer also to the hemorrhage imposed on American taxpayers, to the hatreds engendered among 100 million Arabs, to the terror and bloodshed inflicted on Palestinians and non-combattent residents of Lebanon, and to disillusionment of the ideals attributed to America's founding fathers necessary to maintain the state of Israel in a location selected on the basis of unverified reports that an unverifiable "God-up-there" gave the land of Canaan to the children of Israel to occupy and to rule independently forever. Here questions of human rights, humaneness, international law, and fair play are swept aside in favor of doctrinaire Biblical fundamentalism. One could accept as at least as plausible the statement, "Our great leader who lived 3,200 years ago, the prophet Moses, told us to take it, so we did," and argue the merits of the matter from there.

We have argued that Bible and Quran, and numerous other revered and respected works closely associated with those two, are highly meritorious as human documents, though not uniformly so. They are that, but inherently *not* sacrosanct. Even if spoken by God, the messages were received by human beings and transmitted through other human beings. Statements in them alleged to be words of God spoken to his chosen representatives on Earth (chiefly Moses and Muhammad) include admonitions of highest spiritual merit, conducive to peace and goodwill among all people and to serenity and security within the minds of individuals who believe and practice them. They include trivia irrelevant to human behavior or well-being. They include self-serving propaganda intended to promote some one individual or group at the expense of others.

They also include (especially the Bible) much very interesting historical material, again of unequal dependability but providing rich challenges in historical detective work.

The discipline of theology, which to its credit now allies with itself other social sciences, probably includes individuals whose suspicions about the non-sacrosanctity of God's word parallels our own. In general, however, the discipline depends for its very existence on the premise that there is a real entity out there, non-substantial in the sense of not having molecular structure and not being confined to any one location, but anthropomorphic in the sense of planning and doing what He planned, designing and making what he had designed, talking, listening to, and sometimes answering prayer, even setting aside of natural law by an act of His volition—and so forth and so on.

A hundred years ago the philosopher Nietzsche said (or is reported as having said), "God is dead." As with other things which Nietzsche said or is reported to have said, this saying is starkly quotable, but one wishes to dissociate oneself from the content. Today one would say, "God-out-there is dead but God-in-here is very, very much alive, still very much the arbiter and judge of human affairs. He does indeed preside over a Kingdom of Heaven as spoken of by Christ—in its Earthly presence—and shares of himself, which is to say rules that Kingdom by means of what we define as Holy Spirit, not necessarily as theologians define Holy Spirit."

That would be one manifestation of God-in-here, Deus Sapiens—in this case a very ideal manifestation, somewhat akin perhaps to delineations of Thelème or the Elysian Fields. Other manifestations would be seen in every vital religion ever formulated by human beings anywhere. However, we must remember that, if humans were to cease to exist—for example through having made this planet uninhabitable as a result of over-population or nuclear holocaust, and having failed to establish colonies somewhere else in the universe—then and only then, would God-in-here, Deus Sapiens, cease to exist. However, the universe and Deus Universalis would go on.

One puzzles what to say of the discipline of theology under these circumstances. One can be reasonably sure that old-line theologians will be outraged and speechless—if that is a condition to which theologians are susceptible—at this or any suggestion that they and their discipline are obsolete: consigned to the status of mythologians. Yet that is a very honorable estate. One would find the poet Homer there and the brothers Grimm, Frazer, Campbell, and many others. Mythologians have much to say which enriches our lives and helps us to understand human existence.

To seek knowledge and understanding about the God-in-here

would evoke all of the zest of scientific as well as spiritual quest, and be clothed in all the importance formerly associated with theology as we knew it. Perhaps to this end, theology would merge into a new interdisciplinary "ology" embracing man's religious nature in all its aspects, using scientific methodology to observe human behavior, and adapt existing theories to the realities of observed facts. The new discipline would draw upon all social and physical sciences that can contribute to an understanding of human behavior, including medicine and particularly the neurosciences. All of humankind's rich and beneficial heritage of emotional and religious experience developed over the past several millennia could be preserved and enhanced and made more generally available. Negative elements that have supported theology in the past, that is to say, ignorance, superstition, bigotry and fanaticism, would be recognized as evils by this new discipline and repudiated. These are followers and supporters from whom even the most progressive theology could not entirely free itself as long as it depended upon the concept of an anthropomorphic supra-superman controlling the affairs of human beings from a watchtower somewhere "out there."

Old-line theology carried with it a certain grandeur and mystique, built up over many centuries. In America, especially the United States, many of our most prestigious educational institutions, ivy league colleges and others, were founded by theologians to train younger men for the service of God, and through that service for the moral betterment of men and women of the time. Almost all of these institutions have shed their theological orientation. Many have very distinguished multi-discipline science faculties.

In the nineteenth century, many fine young men and women went forth as to war, fired with eagerness to carry the joys and benefits of Christian civilization into darkest Africa, the Middle East, China, India, and all over the world. The missionary movement still attracts numerous religiously dedicated young people, who perform wonderful services, but mostly in the areas of medicine and health care. Theology itself has had to take a back seat. During much of the medieval and renaissance periods of western history, theologians (partly by reason of being better educated) held many responsible positions in government. The Catholic Church at times functioned as a super-state. Theocracy was the order of the day. Now theocracy (rule in the name of God and in accordance with rules set by God as interpreted by the ruler) is mostly confined to minor situations.

This recalls Rudyard Kipling's solemn and prophetic words in his *Recessional:*

> Far called, our navies melt away.
> On dune and headland sinks the fire:
> Lo, all our pomp of yesterday
> Is one with Ninevah and Tyre!

This may be read as a dirge by old-line theologians and theocrats, and by "pharisees" of all times and all places and all religions, but for those who would enlist the best features of humankind's innate religious nature in the effort to utilize all that science can contribute toward the betterment of the human condition it is not a dirge, it is an emancipation proclamation! It is a welcome to the exciting new world that is being opened up by science! Beyond the question, who made you, still lies the question how are you going to handle its challenges and responsibilities?

Bibliography

Adair, Robert K. "A Flaw in a Universal Mirror: Without a Slight Asymmetry in a "Mirror" Called CP Invariance the Universe as We Know It Would Not Exist; Instead It Would Be Devoid of Matter. What Force in Nature Causes the Flaw?" *Scientific American* 258, no. 2 (February 1988): 50–56.

Adamiak, Richard. *History in the Old Testament: The Evolution of Divine Retribution in the Historiographies of the Wilderness Generation.* Cleveland: John T. Zubal, Inc., 1982.

Albright, William F. *Archaeology and the Religion of Israel.* Baltimore: Johns Hopkins Press, 1942.

_____. "Abraham and the Hebrews: A New Archaeological Interpretation." *Bulletin of ASOR*, no. 163 (1961): 36–54.

_____. *The Biblical Period from Abraham to Ezra: An Historical Survey.* New York: Harper & Row Publishers, 1963.

_____. "The Patriarchs from Abraham to Joseph." Published posthumously in *Biblical Archaeologist* 36, no. 1 (February, 1973): 5–33.

Augustine of Hippo. *City of God.* New York: Doubleday & Co., Inc., 1958.

_____. *Confessions.* New York: Penguin Books, 1961.

Bellah, Robert N. *Beyond Belief: Essays on Religion in a Post-Traditional World.* New York: Harper & Row Publishers, 1970.

Bible. King James Translation. Nonesuch edition. New York: Dial Press, 1924–27.

_____. Nelson's Complete Concordance of the Revised Standard Version. New York: Thomas Nelson & Sons, 1957.

_____. Grant-Rowley Revision of Hastings' Dictionary of the Bible. New York: Charles Scribner's Sons, 1963.

————. New American Standard Translation. La Habra, CA: Foundation Press Publications, 1963.

————. New English Translation. Oxford, Cambridge: 1970.

————. Interpreter's One-Volume Commentary on the Bible. Nashville, Tenn: Abington Press, 1971.

Bulliet, Richard W. *Conversion to Islam in the Medieval Period: An Essay in Quantitative History.* Cambridge, MA: Harvard University Press, 1979.

The Cambridge Ancient History (3rd ed.). Cambridge, England: Cambridge University Press, 1975.

The Cambridge History of Islam (2 vols). Cambridge, England: Cambridge University Press, 1970.

The Cambridge Medieval History. Cambridge, England: Cambridge University Press, 1966.

Campbell, Joseph. *The Masks of God: Occidental Mythology.* New York: Viking Press, 1964.

Crossan, John D. *The Cross That Spoke: The Origins of the Passion Narrative.* San Francisco: Harper & Row, 1988.

Dunlop, Douglas M. *The History of the Jewish Khazars.* Princeton, NJ: Princeton University Press, 1954.

————. *Arab Civilization to A.D. 1500.* New York: Praeger Publishers, 1971.

The Encyclopedia of Islam. Leiden: E. V. Brill, 1960, 1978.

Feuerlicht, Roberta S. *The Fate of the Jews: A People Torn between Israeli Power and Jewish Ethics.* New York: New York Times Books, 1983.

Freud, Sigmund. *Moses and Monotheism.* New York: Alfred Knopf, 1939.

Fromm, Erich. *Escape From Freedom.* New York: Reinhart & Co., 1941.

————. *Man for Himself: An Inquiry into the Psychology of Ethics.* New York: Reinhart & Co., 1947.

————. *Psychoanalysis and Religion.* New Haven, Conn.: Yale University Press, 1950.

Garsoian, Nina G. *The Paulician Hershey.* New York: Columbia University Press, 1967.

Gleick, James. *Chaos: Making a New Science.* New York: The Viking Press, 1987.

Goitein, S. D. *A Medieval Society: The Jewish Communities of the Arab World as Portrayed in the Documents of the Cairo Geniza.* 3 vols. Berkeley, Calif: University of California Press, 1967–78.

Goldziher, Ignaz. *Introduction to Islamic Theology and Law.* Translated by Andras and Hamori. Princeton, NJ: Princeton University Press, 1981.

Grant, Michael. *Herod the Great.* New York: Heritage Press 1971.

Grose, Peter. *Israel in the Mind of America*. New York: Shocken Books, 1984.

Hawking, Stephen W. *A Brief History of Time from the Big Bang to Black Holes*. New York: Bantam Books, 1988.

Hitti, Philip K. *History of the Arabs* (10th ed.). New York: St. Martin's Press, 1970.

———. *Islam—A Way of Life*. Minneapolis, Minn.: University of Minnesota Press, 1970.

Hixon, Lex. *Coming Home: The Experience of Enlightenment in Sacred Traditions*. New York: Doubleday & Co., Inc., 1978.

Hook, Sidney, ed. *Religious Experience and Truth—A Symposium*. New York: New York University Press, 1961.

Ibn Ishaq. *The Life of Muhammad*. Translated by A. Guillaume. Lahore, Pakistan: Oxford University Press, 1974.

James, William. *The Varieties of Religious Experience*. Edited with Introduction by Martin E. Marty. London: Longmans, Green & Co., 1902.

Josephus, Flavius Vespasianus. *The Jewish War*. Translated by G. A. Williamson, revised with a new introduction, notes, and appendices, by E. Mary Smallwood. New York: Penguin Books, 1981.

Kassis, Hanna E. *A Concordance of the Quran*. Berkeley, Calif.: University of California Press, 1983.

Katsch, Abraham I. *Judaism in Islam: Biblical and Talmudic Background of the Quran and Its Commentaries* (3rd ed). New York: Spencer-Herman Press, 1980.

Kbner, Amos. "Underground Hiding Complexes from the Barkokhba War in the Judean Shephaleh." *Biblical Archaeologist* 46, no. 4, (December 1983): 210–221.

Keller, Werner. *The Bible as History* (2nd revised ed). New York: William Morrow & Co., 1981.

Kenyon, Kathleen M. *The Bible and Recent Archaeology*. London: The British Museum (Colonade), 1978.

Ladurie, Emmanuel Le Roy. *Montaillou: The Promised Land of Error*. Translated by Barbara Bray. New York: George Braziller, Inc., 1978.

Lammens, H. *Islam: Beliefs and Institutions*. London: Frank Cass & Co., Ltd., 1929.

Lewis, Bernard. *The Assassins: A Radical Sect in Islam*. New York: Basic Books, 1968.

———. *Islam in History: Ideas, Men and Events in the Middle East*. New York: The Library Press, 1973.

———. *History—Remembered, Recovered, Invented*. Princeton, NJ: Princeton University Press, 1975.

_____. *The Origins of Ismal'ilism: A Study of the Historical Background of the Fatamid Caliphate*. New York: AMS, 1975.

Munro, Dana Carleton. *The Kingdom of the Crusaders*. New York: Appleton-Century, 1935.

The New Columbia Encyclopedia. New York: Columbia University Press, 1975.

New Larousse Encyclopedia of Mythologies. New York: Prometheus Press (by arrangement with Libraire Larousse, Paris): 1968.

Omar Khayyam. *Rubaiyat*. A. V. Arberry, trans. London: Emery Walker, Ltd., 1949.

_____. *Rubaiyat*. E. H. Whinfield, trans. London: Octagon Press for the Sufi Trust, 1980.

_____. *Rubaiyat*. Comparative texts of the five editions. Cecile Mactaggart (private edition): London, 1984.

Ostrogorsky, George. *History of the Byzantine State*. New Brunswick: Rutgers University Press, 1965.

Pagels, Elaine. *The Gnostic Gospels*. New York: Random House, 1979.

Pagels, Heinz R. *Perfect Symmetry: The Search for the Beginning of Time*. New York: Simon & Schuster, 1985.

Pedley, Timothy A., M.D. "Brain, Nerve, and Muscle Disorders," in *The Columbia University College of Physicians and Surgeons Complete Home Medical Guide*. New York: Crown Publishers, 1985.

Perowne, Stewart. *The Later Herods: The Political Background of the New Testament*. Nashville, Tenn. and New York: Abingdon Press, 1958.

Prigogine, Ilya, and Stengers, Isabelle. *Order Out of Chaos: Man's New Dialogue with Nature*. New York: Bantam Books, 1984.

Quran. Translated by A. J. Arberry. New York: Macmillan Co., Inc., 1970.

_____. Translated by N. J. Dawood (4th revised edition), Hamondsworth, Middlesex, England: Penguin Books, Ltd., 1974.

Raven, Charles E. *Natural Religion and Christian Theology*. The Gifford Lectures 1951 & 1952. 2 vols. Cambridge: Cambridge University Press, 1953.

Rensch, Bernard. *Homo Sapiens: From Man to Demigod*. New York: Columbia University Press, 1972.

Ross, Nancy Wilson. *Three Ways of Asian Wisdom: Hinduism, Buddhism, Zen, and Their Significance for the West*. New York: Simon & Schuster, 1966.

Runciman, Steven. *A History of the Crusades* (3 vols). Cambridge: Cambridge University Press, 1951, 1952, 1954.

Salibi, Kamal. *The Bible Came from Arabia*. London: Jonathan Cape, Ltd., 1985.

Schramm, David N., and Steigman, Gary. "Particle Accelerators Test

Cosmological Theory: Is There a Limit to the Number of Families of Elementary Particles." *Scientific American* 258, no. 6 (June 1988): 66–72.

Schroeder, Eric. *Muhammad's People: A Tale by Anthology—The Religion and Politics, Poetry and Violence, Science, Ribaldry & Finance of the Muslims from the Age of Ignorance before Islam and the Mission of God's Prophet to Sophistication in the Eleventh Century.* Portland, Maine: The Bond Wheelwright Co., 1955.

Schwarz, Leo W., ed. *Great Ages & Ideas of the Jewish People.* New York: Modern Library, 1956.

Seaver, George. *Albert Schweitzer: Christian Revolutionary.* New York: Harper & Brothers, 1944.

Setton, Kenneth M., ed. *A History of the Crusades* (6 vols). Madison: The University of Wisconsin Press, 1969.

Settzer, Leon E., ed. *The Columbia Lippincott Gazetteer of the World.* New York: Columbia University Press, 1960.

Smith, Margaret. *Studies in Early Mysticism in the Near and Middle East.* London: Sheldon Press, 1931.

Strayer, Joseph R. *The Albigensian Crusades.* New York: Dial Press, 1971.

Van Seters, John. *The Hyksos: A New Investigation.* New Haven, Conn.: Yale University Press, 1966.

Warner, Marina. *Alone of All Her Sex: The Myth and Cult of the Virgin Mary.* London: George Weidenfield & Nicolson, Ltd., 1976.

Wasson, R. Gordon, Ruck, Carl A. P., and Hoffmann, Albert. *The Road to Eleusis: Unveiling the Secret of the Mysteries.* New York: Harcourt Brace Jovanovich, 1978.

Watt, Montgomery. *Muhammad at Mecca.* Oxford: Oxford University Press, 1953.

————. *Muhammad at Medina.* Oxford: Claredon Press, 1956.

————. *Bell's Introduction to the Quran* (Completely Revised and Enlarged). Edinburgh, Scotland: Edinburgh University Press, 1970.

————. *The Formative Period of Islamic Thought.* Edinburgh, Scotland: Edinburgh University Press, 1973.

Weinberg, Steven. *The First Three Minutes: A Modern View of the Origin of the Universe* (rev. ed.). New York: Basic Books, 1988.

Wender, Paul H., and Klein, Donald F. *Mind, Mood, & Medicine: A Guide to the New Biopsychiatry.* New York: Farrar, Strauss & Giroux, 1981.

Index

About the Author

ALFRED H. HOWELL is a retired banker who graduated from Princeton University in 1934 with an A.B. degree in History. He became interested specifically in the Crusades and the Medieval period in general. After a career in the banking industry and raising a family of one girl and two boys, he took early retirement in 1972 and returned to academia to pursue his interest at Columbia University. Since there were no advanced courses dealing directly with the Crusades from the European point of view, he turned to the Islamic side, receiving an M.A. in Medieval Islamic History in 1976 and an M.Phil. in 1978. Still dissatisfied as to the reasons why so much bloodshed and persecution would be carried on in the name of two religions that basically recognized the same God, he has pursued his inquiries into this matter independently. As it turned out, in his words, the question almost answered itself—following upon the observations recorded in the present work.

About the Founder of This Series

RUTH NANDA ANSHEN, Ph.D., Fellow of the Royal Society of Arts of London, founded, plans, and edits several distinguished series, including World Perspectives, Religious Perspectives, Credo Perspectives, Perspectives in Humanism, the Science of Culture Series, the Tree of Life Series, and Convergence. She also writes and lectures on the relationship of knowledge to the nature and meaning of man and to his understanding of and place in the universe. Dr. Anshen's book, *The Reality of the Devil: Evil in Man*, a study in the phenomenology of evil, demonstrates the interrelationship between good and evil. She is also the author of *Anatomy of Evil* and of *Biography of an Idea*. She has lectured in universities throughout the civilized world on the unity of mind and matter and on the relationship of facts to values. Dr. Anshen is a member of the American Philosophical Association, the History of Science Society, the International Philosophical Society, and the Metaphysical Society of America.